I0797626

WOMEN'S
2026
SOCCER
LEGENDS

PUBLISHED IN THE USA 2025 BY WELBECK CHILDREN'S BOOKS
An imprint of Hachette Children's Group
Part of Hodder & Stoughton Limited
Carmelite House, 50 Victoria Embankment, London, EC4Y 0DZ
An Hachette UK Company
www.hachette.co.uk
www.hachettechildrens.co.uk

All statistical data and player heat maps provided by Opta, under license from Stats Perform.

10 9 8 7 6 5 4 3 2 1
ISBN 978 1 80453 7978
Printed and bound in Dubai
Author: Kevin Pettman
Senior Commissioning Editor: Suhel Ahmed
Design Manager: Matt Drew
Picture research: Paul Langan
Production: Melanie Robertson

PICTURE CREDITS
The publishers would like to thank the following sources for their kind permission to reproduce the pictures in this book.

Getty Images: Eric Alonso 8; ANP 79; Marc Atkins 61; Tnani Badreddine/DeFodi Images 7; Naomi Baker/The FA 59, 78; Ira L. Black/Corbis 106T, 108B, 110B; Bagu Blanco/Pressinphoto/Icon Sport 40; Jose Breton/Pics Action/NurPhoto 16, 21, 77; Alex Broadway/The FA 105; Rico Brouwer/Soccrates 72; Alex Burstow/Arsenal FC 14, 46, 62; Alex Caparros 64; Steph Chambers 108T; Jenny Chuang/ISI Photos 20, 98; Seb Daly/Sportsfile 25; Kelly Defina 109T; Graham Denholm 103; Daniel Derajinski/Icon Sport 110T; Elianton/Mondadori Portfolio 51; Eurasia Sport Images 39; Jacques Feeney/Offside 44, 52; Baptiste Fernandez/Icon Sport 106B; Franck Fife/AFP 35, 85; Foto Olimpik/NurPhoto 73; Craig Foy/SNS Group 102; Nigel French/Sportsphoto/Allstar 15; Scott Gardiner 109B; Gaspafotos/MB Media 99; Edith Geuppert/GES Sportfoto 75; Rich Graessle/Icon Sportswire 101; Alex Grimm 20, 30, 48, 53; Masashi Hara 41; Oliver Hardt 65, 93, 111B; Morgan Harlow/The FA 94; Jose Hernandez/Anadolu Agency 69; Christian Hofer/UEFA 63; Harry How 42; Soobum Im/NWSL 60; Johnnie Izquierdo 82; Jung Yeon-Je/AFP 38; Eddie Keogh/The FA 13; Christof Koepsel 49; Harriet Lander/Chelsea FC 36; Harriet Lander/The FA 56; Roy Lazet/Soccrates 55; Chris Lee/Chelsea FC 97; Christian Liewig/Corbis 27; Warren Little 87; Katharine Lotze 83; Ian MacNicol 57; Carmen Mandato 88; Steven Markham/Icon Sportswire 86; Matt McNulty 107T; Pablo Morano/MB Media 22; Jonathan Moscrop 92; Doug Murray/Icon Sportswire 96; Alex Pantling/UEFA 66; Richard Pelham/The FA 31; Ryan Pierse 9; Daniel Pockett 28; Joe Prior/Visionhaus 10, 54, 67, 71; Manuel Queimadelos/Quality Sport Images 11, 89; David Ramirez/Quality Sport Images 24; David Ramos 5, 34, 45, 70; Chris Ricco 90; Pablo Rodriguez/Quality Sport Images 33; Sandra Ruhaut/Icon Sport 91; Will Russell 12; Pedro Salado 26, 107B; Pedro Salado/Quality Sport Images 29; Richard Sellers/Sportsphoto/Allstar 47, 74; Justin Setterfield 23; Alex Slitz 18; Brad Smith/ISI Photos 76, 80; Diego Souto 50; Janelle St Pierre 68; Rich Storry/NWSL 95; Kenzo Tribouillard/AFP 100; Omar Vega 37; Visionhaus 17, 43, 81; Sebastian Widmann 111T. Shutterstock: Dejan Popovic 104

Every effort has been made to acknowledge correctly and contact the source and/or copyright holder of each picture; any unintentional errors or omissions will be corrected in future editions of this book.

All data correct up to June 2025

WOMEN'S 2026 SOCCER LEGENDS

STATS • PROFILES • TOP PLAYERS

WELBECK
CHILDREN'S BOOKS

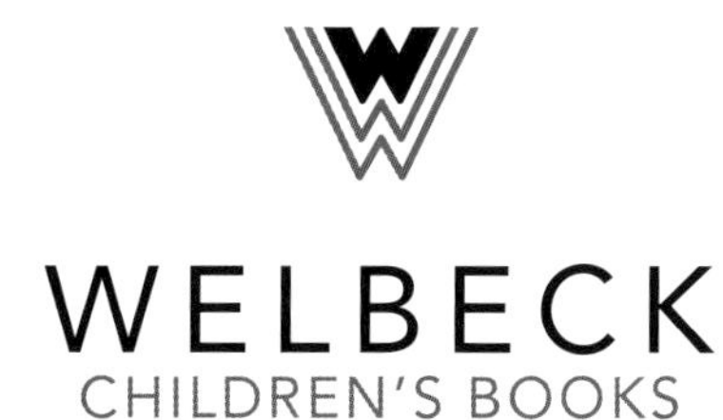

CONTENTS

HOW TO USE THIS BOOK 5

DEFENDERS 6
Ona Batlle 8
Millie Bright 9
Lucy Bronze 10
Olga Carmona 11
Elllie Carpenter 12
Jess Carter 13
Steph Catley 14
Niamh Charles 15
Magdalena Eriksson 16
Emily Fox 17
Vanessa Gilles 18
Naomi Girma 19
Guilia Gwinn 20
Amanda Ilestedt 21
Sakina Karchaoui 22
Ashley Lawrence 23
Mapi León 24
Katie McCabe 25
Irene Paredes 26
Wendie Renard 27
Rebekah Stott 28
Marta Torrejón 29
Glódís Viggósdóttir 30
Leah Williamson 31

MIDFIELDERS 32
Aitana Bonmatí 34
Delphine Cascarino 35
Erin Cuthbert 36
Debinha 37
Melchie Dumornay 38
Grace Geyoro 39
Patri Guijarro 40
Yui Hasegawa 41
Lindsey Heaps 42
Lauren Hemp 43
Kim Little 44
Vicky López 45
Frida Maanum 46
Hinata Miyazawa 47
Sioeke Nüsken 48
Lena Oberdorf 49
Clàudia Pina 50
Alexia Putellas 51
Guro Reiten 52
Georgia Stanway 53
Ella Toone 54
Daniëlle van de Donk 55
Keira Walsh 56
Caroline Weir 57

FORWARDS 58
Barbra Banda 60
Stina Blackstenius 61
Mariona Caldentey 62
Kadidiatou Diani 63
Caroline Graham Hansen 64
Pernille Harder 65
Ada Hegerberg 66
Lauren James 67
Sam Kerr 68
Rachael Kundananji 69
Eugénie Le Sommer 70
Beth Mead 71
Vivianne Miedema 72
Ewa Pajor 73
Salma Paralluelo 74
Alexander Popp 75
Trinity Rodman 76
Fridolina Rolfö 77
Alessia Russo 78
Lea Schüller 79
Jaedyn Shaw 80
Khadija Shaw 81
Mallory Swanson 82
Sophia Wilson (Smith) 83

GOALKEEPERS 84
Mackenzie Arnold 86
Ann-Katrin Berger 87
Jane Campbell 88
Catalina Coll 89
Mary Earps 90
Christiane Endler 91
Merle Frohms 92
Maria Luisa Grohs 93
Hannah Hampton 94
Aubrey Renee Kinsgbury 95
Casey Murphy 96
Zećira Mušović 97
Alyssa Naeher 98
Chiamaka Nnadozie 99
Sandra Paños 100
Kailen Sheridan 101
Daphne Van Domselaar 102
Lydia Williams 103

MANAGERS 104
Juan Carlos Amorós 106
Sonia Bompastor
Jonas Eidevall 107
Jonatan Giráldez
Laura Harvey 108
Seb Hines
Jeff Hopkins 109
Ante Juric
Joe Montemurro 110
Casey Stoney
Alexander Straus 111
Tommy Stroot

HOW TO USE THIS BOOK

Welcome to *Soccer Legends 2026 (Women)*—packed with the latest performance stats of today's top players and coaches in the women's game! We have selected more than 100 stars from the world's best leagues, which includes the National Women's Soccer League (NWSL) in the USA, the Women's Super League (WSL) in England, Australia's A-League, as well as the elite leagues in Spain, France, and Germany. The players and coaches have spent at least the past three seasons of their careers operating in these top leagues. With all the key stats at your fingertips, you can use this book to anaylze their performances and determine whether or not they are currently the most in-form defenders, midfielders, forwards, goalkeepers, and managers in the world.

The types of stats featured for each position vary, because each position performs a specific role on the field. For example, a defender's main job is to stop the opposition from scoring, so the stats focus mainly on this part of the player's game. Likewise, a striker's tackling is not as relevant as their goal or assists tally. What you will find for all the players is their heat map, which shows the areas of the field they focus their play in or, with goalkeepers, whether they prefer to stay in the six-yard box or play more as a "sweeper keeper," moving more freely around the penalty area.

The stats relate to a player's performances over the past three seasons (2022/'23, 2023'/24 and 2024/'25), as members of teams belonging to one of the top leagues. The only exception lies with NWSL players, whose stats span seasons 2022 to 2024, plus the first 10 matches of 2025. The figures have been collected from domestic league and European match appearances (the latter not applying to players in NWSL, of course) and exclude data from domestic cup, super cups, or international games.

DEFENDERS

In elite-level soccer, a defender is much more than a player responsible for stopping the opposition from scoring. While that remains the priority, defenders also help build attacks by bringing the ball out from the back or making a long-range pass. Defensive positions include center-backs, full-backs, and wing-backs. There can be two or three center-backs on a team and they are usually tall, with the power to tackle and height advantage to head the ball away. Full-backs and wing-backs operate in wide areas and they must have the speed, skill, and energy to defend their box and make penetrating forward runs.

WHAT DO THESE STATS MEAN?

AERIAL DUELS WON

This is the percentage of headers a defender has won in her own penalty area to interrupt an opposition attack.

INTERCEPTIONS

The number of times a defender has successfully stopped an attack without needing to make a tackle.

BLOCKS

A shot that is intercepted by a defender—preventing her keeper from having to make a save.

PASS ACCURACY

Pass accuracy indicates, as a percentage, the player's ability to complete a pass to a teammate.

CLEARANCES

An attack successfully foiled, either by kicking or heading the ball away from danger.

TACKLES

The number of times a defender has challenged and dispossessed the opposition without committing a foul.

Did you know?

At the start of the 2024/25 season, Lyon did not concede a goal in the league in their first nine games. Their rock-hard defense is built around the leadership of captain Wendie Renard, who has the height, power, and skills to keep danger from her goal.

ONA BATLLE

Ona Batlle was a Barcelona youth player before developing her attacking and defensive skills at Levante and Manchester United. The right-back rejoined Barça in 2023 and her eye-catching runs and strong tackling have since become a standout feature of her game.

NATIONALITY
Spain

CURRENT CLUB
Barcelona

DATE OF BIRTH	JUN 10, 1999
POSITION	RIGHT-BACK
HEIGHT	5 FT. 5 IN.
PRO DEBUT	2014
PREFERRED FOOT	RIGHT

MAJOR CLUB HONORS

⚽ UEFA Women's Champions League: 2024, runner-up 2025 ⚽ Liga F: 2024, 2025 ⚽ Copa de la Reina: 2017, 2024, 2025 ⚽ Women's FA Cup: Runner-up 2023 (Manchester United)

INTERNATIONAL HONORS

⚽ FIFA Women's World Cup: 2023
⚽ UEFA Women's Nations League: 2024

ACTIVITY AREAS

MILLIE BRIGHT

After spending her early career in midfield, Millie Bright became a center-back, where her accurate passing and clever movement, combined with her powerful heading and interceptions make her immense in defense. She is a strong leader on the field too.

NATIONALITY
England

CURRENT CLUB
Chelsea

DATE OF BIRTH	AUG 21, 1993
POSITION	CENTRAL
HEIGHT	5 FT. 9 IN.
PRO DEBUT	2009
PREFERRED FOOT	RIGHT

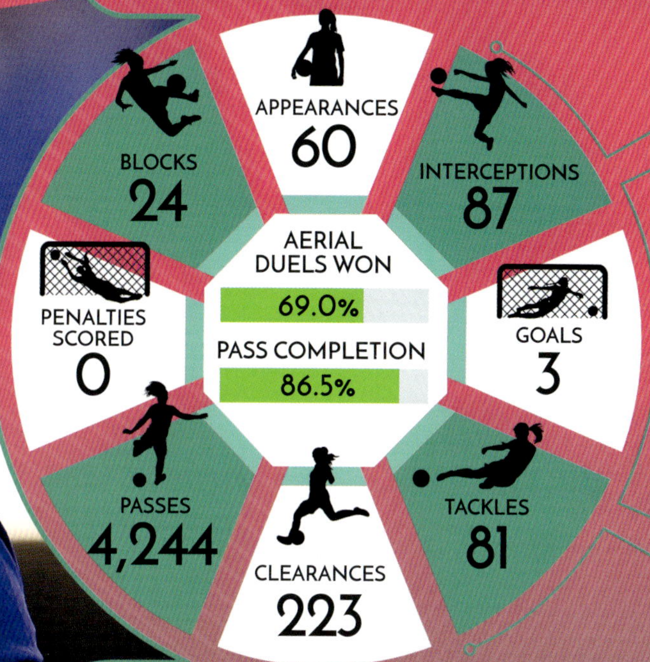

APPEARANCES 60

INTERCEPTIONS 87

GOALS 3

TACKLES 81

CLEARANCES 223

PASSES 4,244

PENALTIES SCORED 0

BLOCKS 24

AERIAL DUELS WON 69.0%

PASS COMPLETION 86.5%

MAJOR CLUB HONORS

⚽ Women's Super League: 2015, 2018, 202, 2021, 2022, 2023, 2024, 2025 ⚽ UEFA Women's Champions League: Runner-up 2021 ⚽ Women's FA Cup: 2015, 2018, 2021, 2022, 2023, 2024, 2025 ⚽ Women's FA League Cup: 2020, 2021, 2025

INTERNATIONAL HONORS

⚽ UEFA Women's Championship: 2022
⚽ FIFA Women's World Cup: Runner-up 2023

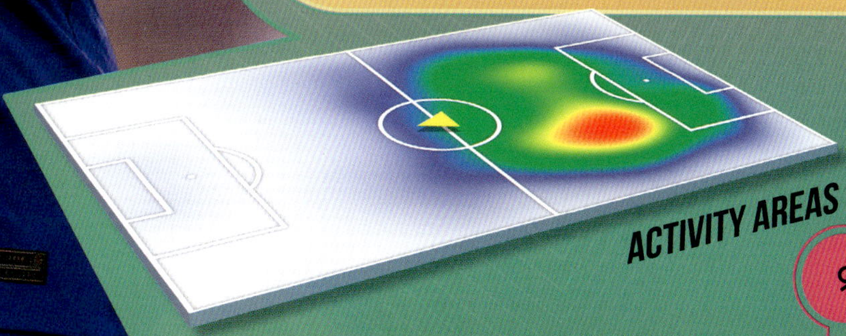

ACTIVITY AREAS

LUCY BRONZE

For more than a decade now, Lucy Bronze has been among the best full-backs in world soccer. She's known for her energy, clean tackling, and bursting right-wing raids. What's more, she has a knack for scoring headers from free-kicks and corners.

NATIONALITY
England

CURRENT CLUB
Chelsea

DATE OF BIRTH	OCT 28, 1991
POSITION	RIGHT-BACK
HEIGHT	5 FT. 8 IN.
PRO DEBUT	2007
PREFERRED FOOT	RIGHT

MAJOR CLUB HONORS

⚽ Liga F: 2023, 2024 ⚽ UEFA W. Champions League: 2023, 2024 (all Barça), 2018*, 2019*, 2020* (*Lyon), 2024 (Barça) ⚽ Division 1 Féminine: 2018, 2019, 2020 (all Lyon) ⚽ WSL: 2013, 2014* (*Liverpool), 2016, (Man. City), 2025 ⚽ Women's FA Cup: 2025 ⚽ Coupe de France Féminine: 2019, 2020 (all Lyon)

INTERNATIONAL HONORS

- UEFA Women's Championship: 2022
- FIFA Women's World Cup: Runner-up 2023
- Women's Finalissima: 2023

OLGA CARMONA

Scoring the winning goals in both the semifinal and final of the 2023 FIFA World Cup catapulted Olga Carmona to global stardom. A stylish defender, when Carmona dispossesses an opponent, expect to see her power forward with the ball and test the goalkeeper or expertly pick out a teammate.

NATIONALITY
Spain

CURRENT CLUB
Real Madrid

DATE OF BIRTH	DEC 06, 2000
POSITION	LEFT-BACK
HEIGHT	5 FT. 3 IN.
PRO DEBUT	2017
PREFERRED FOOT	LEFT

APPEARANCES 97

INTERCEPTIONS 130

GOALS 17

TACKLES 198

CLEARANCES 73

PASSES 3,831

PENALTIES SCORED 9

BLOCKS 9

AERIAL DUELS WON 45.2%

PASS COMPLETION 79.3%

MAJOR CLUB HONORS
- None to date

INTERNATIONAL HONORS
- FIFA Women's World Cup: 2023
- UEFA Women's Nations League: 2024

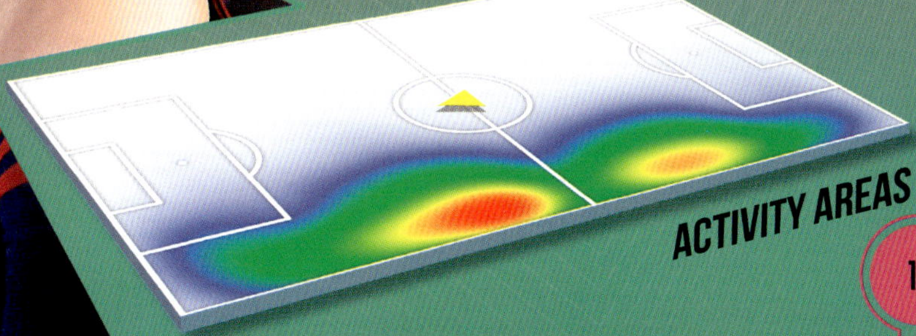

ACTIVITY AREAS

NATIONALITY
Australia

CURRENT CLUB
Lyon

ELLIE CARPENTER

Ever reliable at the back, Ellie Carpenter can shut down attacks in her box with great speed. She's also adept at making overlapping runs and cleverly pulling opponents out of position, which makes her a menace at the attacking end of the field.

DATE OF BIRTH	APR 28, 2000
POSITION	RIGHT-BACK
HEIGHT	1.64 M
PRO DEBUT	2015
PREFERRED FOOT	RIGHT

APPEARANCES	64
INTERCEPTIONS	48
GOALS	2
TACKLES	109
CLEARANCES	50
PASSES	2,962
PENALTIES SCORED	0
BLOCKS	7
AERIAL DUELS WON	26.0%
PASS COMPLETION	86.0%

MAJOR CLUB HONORS

⚽ Première Ligue (Division 1 Féminine): 2022, 2023, 2024, 2025 ⚽ UEFA W. Champions League: 2020, 2022, runner-up 2024 ⚽ Coupe de France Féminine: 2020, 2023 ⚽ A-League Premiership: 2020 (Melbourne City) ⚽ A-League Championship: 2020 (Melbourne City)

INTERNATIONAL HONORS

⚽ None to date

ACTIVITY AREAS

JESS CARTER

Jess Carter's versatility means she can play across the defensive line and even in midfield. Robust in possession and with quick acceleration, she enjoys battles against tall strikers and speedy wingers, frequently winning those clashes.

NATIONALITY
England

CURRENT CLUB
Gotham FC

27

DATE OF BIRTH	27 OCT, 1997
POSITION	CENTRAL
HEIGHT	5 FT. 5 IN.
PRO DEBUT	2013
PREFERRED FOOT	RIGHT

MAJOR CLUB HONORS

⚽ Women's Super League: 2020, 2021, 2022, 2023, 2024 (all Chelsea) ⚽ UEFA Women's Champions League: Runner-up 2021 (Chelsea) ⚽ Women's FA Cup: 2021, 2022, 2023 (all Chelsea) ⚽ Women's FA League Cup: 2020, 2021 (all Chelsea)

INTERNATIONAL HONORS

⚽ UEFA Women's Championship: 2022
⚽ FIFA Women's World Cup: Runner-up 2023
⚽ Women's Finalissima: 2023

ACTIVITY AREAS

NATIONALITY
Australia

CURRENT CLUB
Arsenal

STEPH CATLEY

The Australian Steph Catley is dynamic down the left wing. She will routinely collect the ball in tight defensive positions and coolly play out or make a superb cross-field pass. Her delivery from set pieces regularly sets up scoring chances.

DATE OF BIRTH	JAN 26, 1994
POSITION	LEFT-BACK
HEIGHT	5 FT. 7 IN.
PRO DEBUT	2009
PREFERRED FOOT	LEFT

APPEARANCES 76

BLOCKS 22

INTERCEPTIONS 35

AERIAL DUELS WON 51.1%

PASS COMPLETION 88.0%

PENALTIES SCORED 0

GOALS 2

PASSES 3,629

CLEARANCES 161

TACKLES 73

MAJOR CLUB HONORS
⚽ UEFA Women's Champions League: 2025 ⚽ A-League Championship: 2014 (Melbourne Victory), 2016, 2017, 2018, 2020 (all Melbourne City) ⚽ A-League Premiership: 2016, 2020 (Melbourne City) ⚽ Women's FA Cup: 2023 ⚽ Women's FA League Cup: 2023, 2024

INTERNATIONAL HONORS
⚽ None to date

ACTIVITY AREAS

NIAMH CHARLES

Disciplined at the back and with strong leadership qualities, Niamh Charles is a bedrock in defense. Able to play on both flanks, she is known for passing and crossing well with either foot, darting inside, or even sprinting down the touchline to set up attacks.

NATIONALITY
England

CURRENT CLUB
Chelsea

DATE OF BIRTH	JUN 21, 1999
POSITION	FULL-BACK
HEIGHT	5 FT. 8 IN.
PRO DEBUT	2016
PREFERRED FOOT	RIGHT

APPEARANCES 77

INTERCEPTIONS 84

GOALS 7

TACKLES 167

CLEARANCES 105

PASSES 3,380

PENALTIES SCORED 0

BLOCKS 11

AERIAL DUELS WON 68.1%

PASS COMPLETION 79.7%

MAJOR CLUB HONORS

- Women's Super League: 2021, 2022, 2023, 2024, 2025
- UEFA Women's Champions League: Runner-up 2021
- Women's FA Cup: 2021, 2022, 2023, 2025
- Women's FA League Cup: 2021, 2025

INTERNATIONAL HONORS

- FIFA Women's World Cup: Runner-up 2023
- Women's Finalissima: 2023

ACTIVITY AREAS

NATIONALITY
Sweden

CURRENT CLUB
Bayern Munich

MAGDALENA ERIKSSON

Somehow Magdalena Eriksson improves season after season to add to her reputation as an elite center-back. She is calm in possession, strong in the air, and capable of pinging laser-guided passes that break opposition defenses.

DATE OF BIRTH	SEP 08, 1993
POSITION	CENTRAL
HEIGHT	5 FT. 8 IN.
PRO DEBUT	2011
PREFERRED FOOT	LEFT

APPEARANCES 60
INTERCEPTIONS 61
GOALS 9
TACKLES 58
CLEARANCES 146
PASSES 3,556
PENALTIES SCORED 0
BLOCKS 27

AERIAL DUELS WON 53.2%
PASS COMPLETION 85.7%

MAJOR CLUB HONORS

⚽ Frauen-Bundesliga: 2024, 2025 ⚽ Women's Super League: 2018, 2020, '21, '22, '23 (all Chelsea) ⚽ DFB-Pokal Frauen: 2025 ⚽ Women's FA Cup: 2018, 2021, 2022, 2023 (all Chelsea) ⚽ Women's Champions League: Runner-up 2021 (Chelsea)

INTERNATIONAL HONORS

⚽ FIFA Women's World Cup: Third place 2019, third place 2023 ⚽ Summer Olympic Games: Silver 2016, silver 2020 (2021)

ACTIVITY AREAS

EMILY FOX

Emily Fox moved to the WSL in 2024, raising her already high standards to even greater heights. A strong tackler and assured header defending crosses into her penalty box, Fox also makes overlapping attacking runs that stretch the opposition at the other end of the field.

NATIONALITY
USA

CURRENT CLUB
Arsenal

DATE OF BIRTH	DEC 05, 1998
POSITION	RIGHT-BACK
HEIGHT	5 FT. 5 IN.
PRO DEBUT	2021
PREFERRED FOOT	RIGHT

APPEARANCES 77

INTERCEPTIONS 82

GOALS 6

TACKLES 114

CLEARANCES 153

PASSES 4,006

PENALTIES SCORED 0

BLOCKS 12

AERIAL DUELS WON 53.0%

PASS COMPLETION 85.8%

MAJOR CLUB HONORS
- UEFA Women's Champions League: 2025
- Women's FA League Cup: 2024
- NWSL Challenge Cup: 2023 (North Carolina Courage)

INTERNATIONAL HONORS
- Summer Summer Olympic Games: Gold 2024
- CONCACAF Women's Championship: 2022
- CONCACAF Women's Gold Cup: 2024

ACTIVITY AREAS

NATIONALITY
Canada

CURRENT CLUB
Bayern Munich

VANESSA GILLES

A stellar center-back in the women's game, Vanessa Gilles is superb at winning one-on-ones, outjumping strikers, and knowing exactly when to slide tackle. Her upper-body strength and fearless approach to defending gives her club and country a formidable barrier.

DATE OF BIRTH	MAR 11, 1996
POSITION	CENTRAL
HEIGHT	5 FT. 9 IN.
PRO DEBUT	2017
PREFERRED FOOT	RIGHT

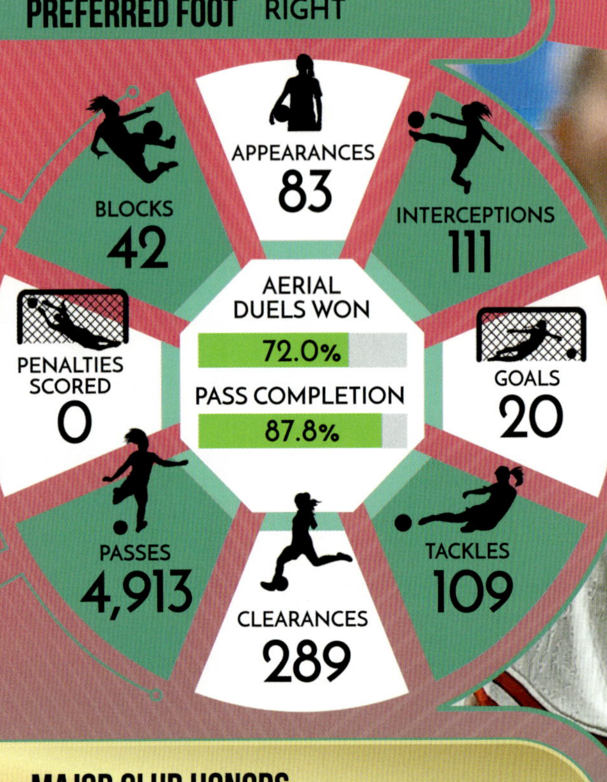

MAJOR CLUB HONORS

- Division 1 Féminine: 2023, 2024, 2025 (all Lyon)
- Coupe de France Féminine: 2023 (Lyon)
- UEFA Women's Champions League: Runner-up 2024 (Lyon)

INTERNATIONAL HONORS

- Summer Olympic Games: Gold 2020 (2021)

ACTIVITY AREAS

NAOMI GIRMA

Naomi Girma has made a rapid rise in world soccer. She reads the game brilliantly, knowing when to step in and make a challenge, which makes her tough to beat. Her consistent performances saw her scoop the NWSL Defender of the Year prize twice before she moved to the WSL in 2025.

NATIONALITY
USA

CURRENT CLUB
Chelsea

DATE OF BIRTH	JUN 14, 2000
POSITION	CENTRAL
HEIGHT	5 FT. 6 IN.
PRO DEBUT	2022
PREFERRED FOOT	RIGHT

APPEARANCES 68

INTERCEPTIONS 65

BLOCKS 59

AERIAL DUELS WON 51.6%

PASS COMPLETION 88.5%

PENALTIES SCORED 0

GOALS 0

PASSES 3,897

CLEARANCES 306

TACKLES 101

MAJOR CLUB HONORS

- NWSL Shield: 2023 (San Diego Wave)
- NWSL Challenge Cup: 2024 (San Diego Wave)
- Women's Super League: 2025
- Women's FA Cup: 2025

INTERNATIONAL HONORS

- CONCACAF Women's Gold Cup: 2024
- CONCACAF Women's Championship: 2022
- Summer Olympic Games: Gold 2024

ACTIVITY AREAS

GUILIA GWINN

After bagging the Best Young Player Award at the 2019 Women's World Cup, Guilia Gwinn has continued to improve for both club and country. A solid and skillful presence in defense, Gwinn also has the ability to launch speedy counterattacks down the wing.

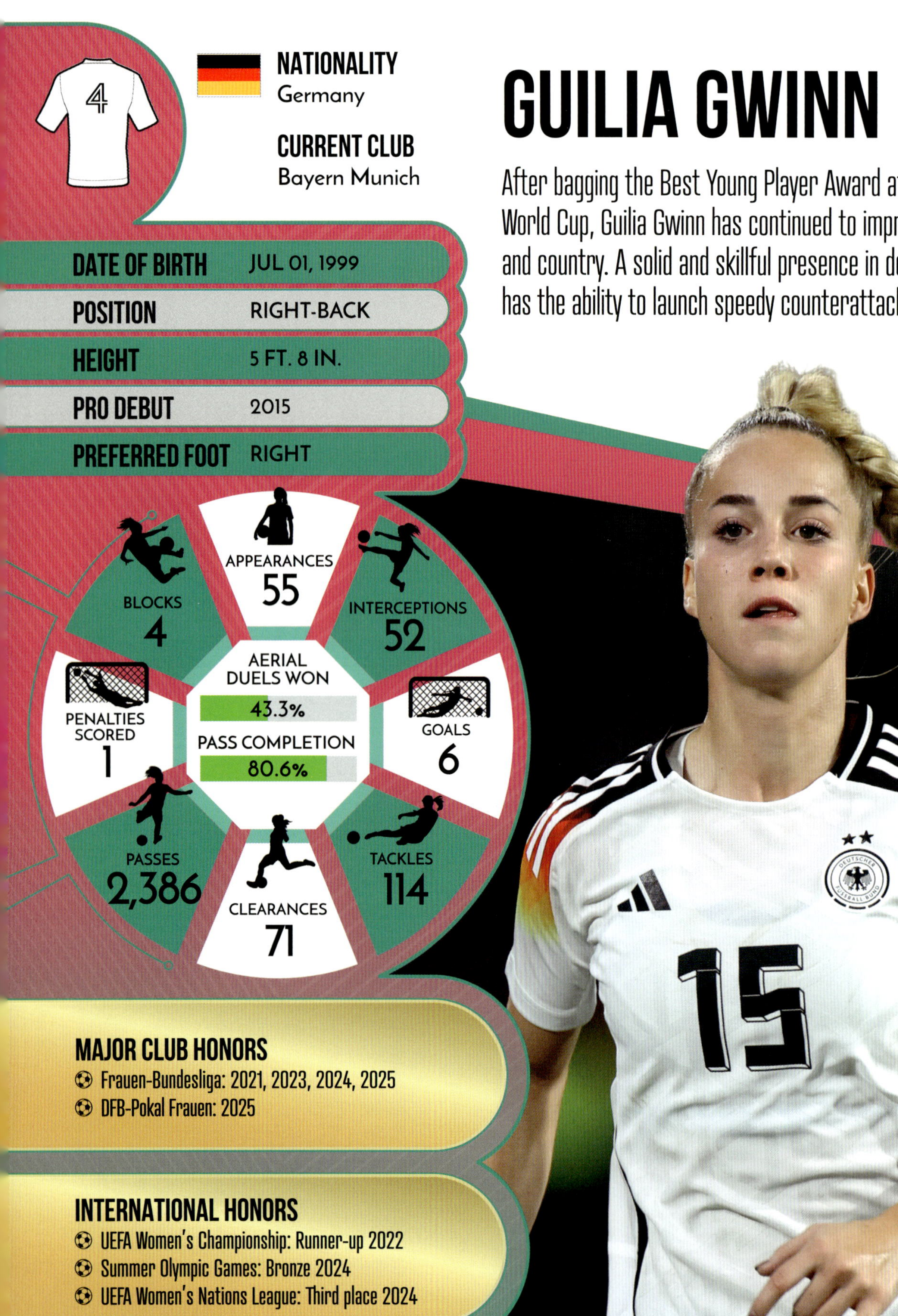

NATIONALITY
Germany

CURRENT CLUB
Bayern Munich

DATE OF BIRTH	JUL 01, 1999
POSITION	RIGHT-BACK
HEIGHT	5 FT. 8 IN.
PRO DEBUT	2015
PREFERRED FOOT	RIGHT

APPEARANCES 55
INTERCEPTIONS 52
GOALS 6
TACKLES 114
CLEARANCES 71
PASSES 2,386
PENALTIES SCORED 1
BLOCKS 4

AERIAL DUELS WON 43.3%
PASS COMPLETION 80.6%

MAJOR CLUB HONORS

- Frauen-Bundesliga: 2021, 2023, 2024, 2025
- DFB-Pokal Frauen: 2025

INTERNATIONAL HONORS

- UEFA Women's Championship: Runner-up 2022
- Summer Olympic Games: Bronze 2024
- UEFA Women's Nations League: Third place 2024

ACTIVITY AREAS

AMANDA ILESTEDT

Amanda Ilestedt is so difficult to beat in the air, using her height, power, and impressive technique to win headers in both penalty boxes. She is hard to dispossess with the ball at her feet and makes difficult passes look simple. She left Arsenal in 2025 after two seasons.

NATIONALITY
Sweden

CURRENT CLUB
TBC

DATE OF BIRTH	JAN 17, 1993
POSITION	CENTRAL
HEIGHT	5 FT. 10 IN.
PRO DEBUT	2008
PREFERRED FOOT	RIGHT

MAJOR CLUB HONORS

⚽ Frauen-Bundesliga: 2021 (Bayern Munich) ⚽ UEFA Women's Champions League: 2025 (Arsenal) ⚽ Coupe de France Féminine: 2022 (PSG) ⚽ Damallsvenskan: 2010, 2011, 2013, 2014 (all FC Rosengard)

INTERNATIONAL HONORS

⚽ Summer Olympic Games: Silver 2016
⚽ FIFA Women's World Cup: Third place 2019, third place 2023

ACTIVITY AREAS

SAKINA KARCHAOUI

A defender who takes pride in keeping clean sheets, Sakina Karchaoui plays like a winger carrying a goal scoring threat. Her wide runs stretch the opposition and she is then able to deliver the ball to a teammate in a prime spot inside the box.

7

NATIONALITY
France

CURRENT CLUB
Paris Saint-Germain

DATE OF BIRTH	JAN 26, 1996
POSITION	LEFT-BACK
HEIGHT	5 FT. 3 IN.
PRO DEBUT	2012
PREFERRED FOOT	LEFT

APPEARANCES 69
INTERCEPTIONS 108
GOALS 8
TACKLES 108
CLEARANCES 51
PASSES 4,087
PENALTIES SCORED 1
BLOCKS 7

AERIAL DUELS WON 53.0%
PASS COMPLETION 82.7%

MAJOR CLUB HONORS

- Coupe de France: 2022, 2024, runner-up 2025
- UEFA Women's Champions League: 2020 (Lyon)

INTERNATIONAL HONORS

- None to date

ACTIVITY AREAS

ASHLEY LAWRENCE

Ashley Lawrence is such a valuable team player because she can play both at left- and right-back. While drilled at keeping danger away from her own box, the defender can also inject creativity and flair into the team with her speedy forward runs and accurate crosses.

NATIONALITY
Canada

CURRENT CLUB
Chelsea

12

DATE OF BIRTH	JUN 11, 1995
POSITION	RIGHT/LEFT
HEIGHT	5 FT. 6 IN.
PRO DEBUT	2013
PREFERRED FOOT	RIGHT

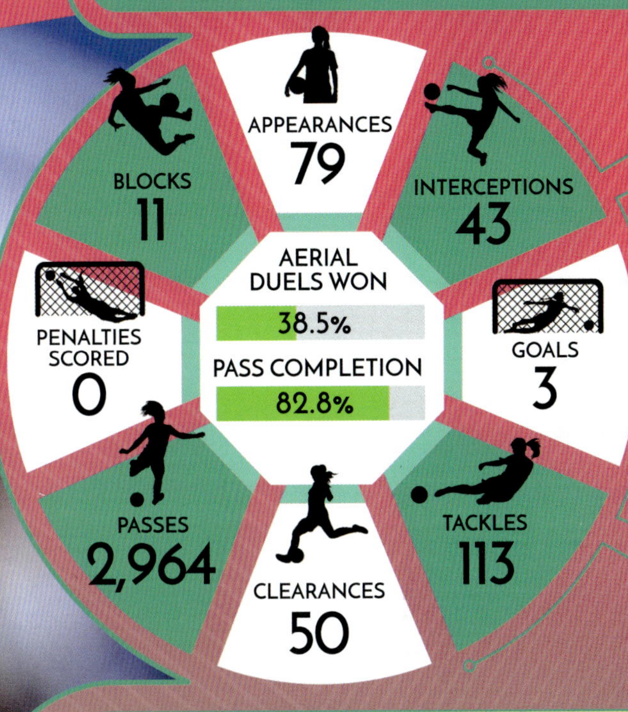

MAJOR CLUB HONORS

⚽ Women's Super League: 2024, 2025 ⚽ Division 1 Féminine: 2021 (PSG) ⚽ Coupe de France: 2018, 2022 (all PSG) ⚽ UEFA Women's Champions League: Runner-up 2017 (PSG) ⚽ Women's FA Cup: 2025 ⚽ FA Women's League Cup: 2025

INTERNATIONAL HONORS

⚽ Summer Olympic Games: Gold 2020 (2021)

ACTIVITY AREAS

MAPI LEÓN

A tough center-back who makes hard but fair challenges with her head and feet, Mapi León is a leader in defense. Playing a high press, she has the confidence to control her line and spring attacks with a telling pass from her cultured left foot.

MAJOR CLUB HONORS

⚽ Liga F: 2017 (Atlético Madrid) 2020, 2021, 2022, 2023, 2024, 2025 ⚽ UEFA Women's Champions League: 2021, 2023, 2024, runner-up 2025 ⚽ Copa de la Reina: 2016 (Atlético Madrid), 2018, 2020, 2021, 2022, 2024, 2025

INTERNATIONAL HONORS

⚽ None to date

KATIE MCCABE

While a stalwart in defense, Katie McCabe is blessed with the technique and determination to cover so much of the field. Her forward runs are perfectly timed and there are not many players who hit left-footed shots quite as sweetly.

NATIONALITY
Republic of Ireland

CURRENT CLUB
Arsenal

DATE OF BIRTH	SEP 21, 1995
POSITION	LEFT BACK
HEIGHT	5 FT. 6 IN.
PRO DEBUT	2011
PREFERRED FOOT	LEFT

MAJOR CLUB HONORS
⚽ Women's Super League: 2019 ⚽ UEFA Women's Champions League: 2025 ⚽ Women's FA Cup: 2016 ⚽ Women's FA League Cup: 2018, 2023, 2024

INTERNATIONAL HONORS
⚽ None to date

ACTIVITY AREAS

IRENE PAREDES

NATIONALITY
Spain

CURRENT CLUB
Barcelona

Few players are better than Irene Paredes when it comes to making a well-timed interception and using flair and vision to deliver the ball to a teammate in an attacking position. The dominant center-back uses her physique to marshall her defensive zone and connect with corners at the other end.

DATE OF BIRTH	JUL 04, 1991
POSITION	CENTRAL
HEIGHT	5 FT. 10 IN.
PRO DEBUT	2008
PREFERRED FOOT	RIGHT

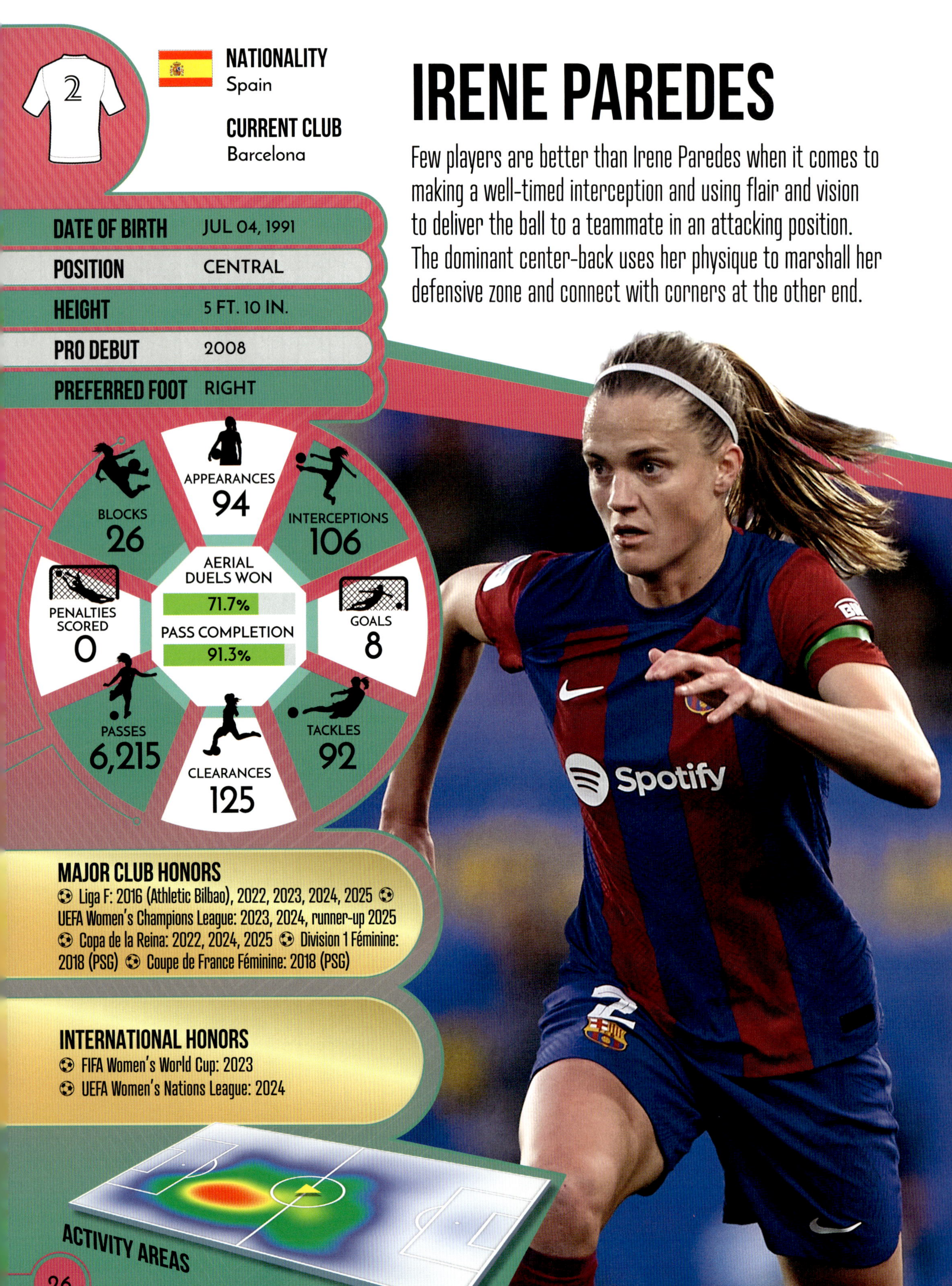

MAJOR CLUB HONORS
⚽ Liga F: 2016 (Athletic Bilbao), 2022, 2023, 2024, 2025 ⚽ UEFA Women's Champions League: 2023, 2024, runner-up 2025 ⚽ Copa de la Reina: 2022, 2024, 2025 ⚽ Division 1 Féminine: 2018 (PSG) ⚽ Coupe de France Féminine: 2018 (PSG)

INTERNATIONAL HONORS
⚽ FIFA Women's World Cup: 2023
⚽ UEFA Women's Nations League: 2024

ACTIVITY AREAS

WENDIE RENARD

The towering Wendie Renard has a trophy cabinet that befits her status as a world-class player. She uses her tall frame and athletic skills to defend her goal and moves like a sprinter when she has to track back or give chase. For more than a decade she has been a gamewinner for both club and country.

NATIONALITY
France

CURRENT CLUB
Lyon

DATE OF BIRTH	JUL 20, 1990
POSITION	CENTRAL
HEIGHT	6 FT. 2 IN.
PRO DEBUT	2006
PREFERRED FOOT	RIGHT

APPEARANCES 75
INTERCEPTIONS 95
GOALS 21
TACKLES 75
CLEARANCES 164
PASSES 4,540
PENALTIES SCORED 4
BLOCKS 19

AERIAL DUELS WON 80.4%
PASS COMPLETION 87.9%

MAJOR CLUB HONORS
⚽ Première Ligue (Division 1 Féminine): 2007–2025 (x18) ⚽ UEFA Champions League: 2011, 2012, 2016, 2017, 2018, 2019, 2020, 2022, runner-up, 2024 ⚽ Coupe de France: 2008, 2012–2017, 2019, 2020, 2023

INTERNATIONAL HONORS
⚽ None to date

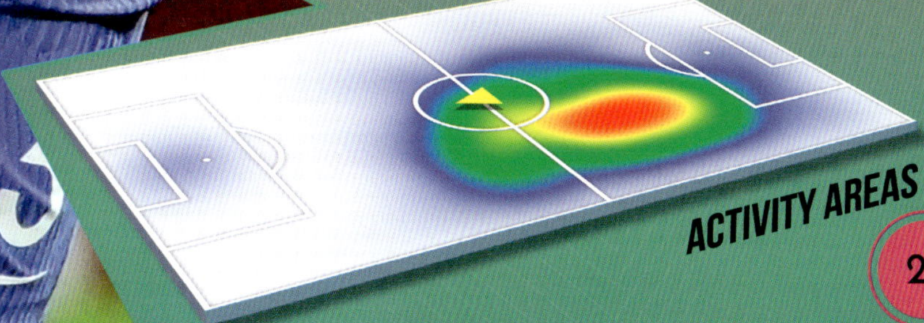

ACTIVITY AREAS

NATIONALITY
New Zealand

CURRENT CLUB
Melbourne City

REBEKAH STOTT

With more than a century of international and A-League (formerly W-League) appearances, Rebekah Stott always delivers influential displays. Superb at reading and breaking up play, she can follow that up with her top quality passing once the ball is at her feet.

DATE OF BIRTH	JUN 17, 1993
POSITION	CENTRAL
HEIGHT	5 FT. 8 IN.
PRO DEBUT	2010
PREFERRED FOOT	RIGHT

APPEARANCES	49
INTERCEPTIONS	92
GOALS	1
TACKLES	76
CLEARANCES	193
PASSES	3,630
PENALTIES SCORED	0
BLOCKS	34
AERIAL DUELS WON	43.5%
PASS COMPLETION	85.2%

MAJOR CLUB HONORS
⚽ A-League Championship: 2011 (Brisbane Roar), 2016, 2017, 2018, 2020 ⚽ A-League Premiership: 2016, 2020

INTERNATIONAL HONORS
⚽ None to date

ACTIVITY AREAS

MARTA TORREJÓN

During a career spent mostly with Barcelona, Marta Torrejón has established herself as a valued member because she can play across the defense. Whether heading balls clear at center-back or attacking from full-back, her impact has driven Barça to multiple domestic and European successes.

NATIONALITY
Spain

CURRENT CLUB
Barcelona

DATE OF BIRTH	FEB 27, 1990
POSITION	CENTRAL
HEIGHT	5 FT. 7 IN.
PRO DEBUT	2004
PREFERRED FOOT	RIGHT

MAJOR CLUB HONORS

⚽ Liga F: 2006 (Espanyol), 2014, 2015, 2020, 2021, 2022, 2023, 2024, 2025 ⚽ UEFA Women's Champions League: 2021, 2023, 2024, runner-up 2025 ⚽ Copa de la Reina: 2006, 2009, 2010, 2012 (all Espanyol), 2014, 2017, 2018, 2020, 2021, 2022, 2024, 2025

INTERNATIONAL HONORS

⚽ None to date

ACTIVITY AREAS

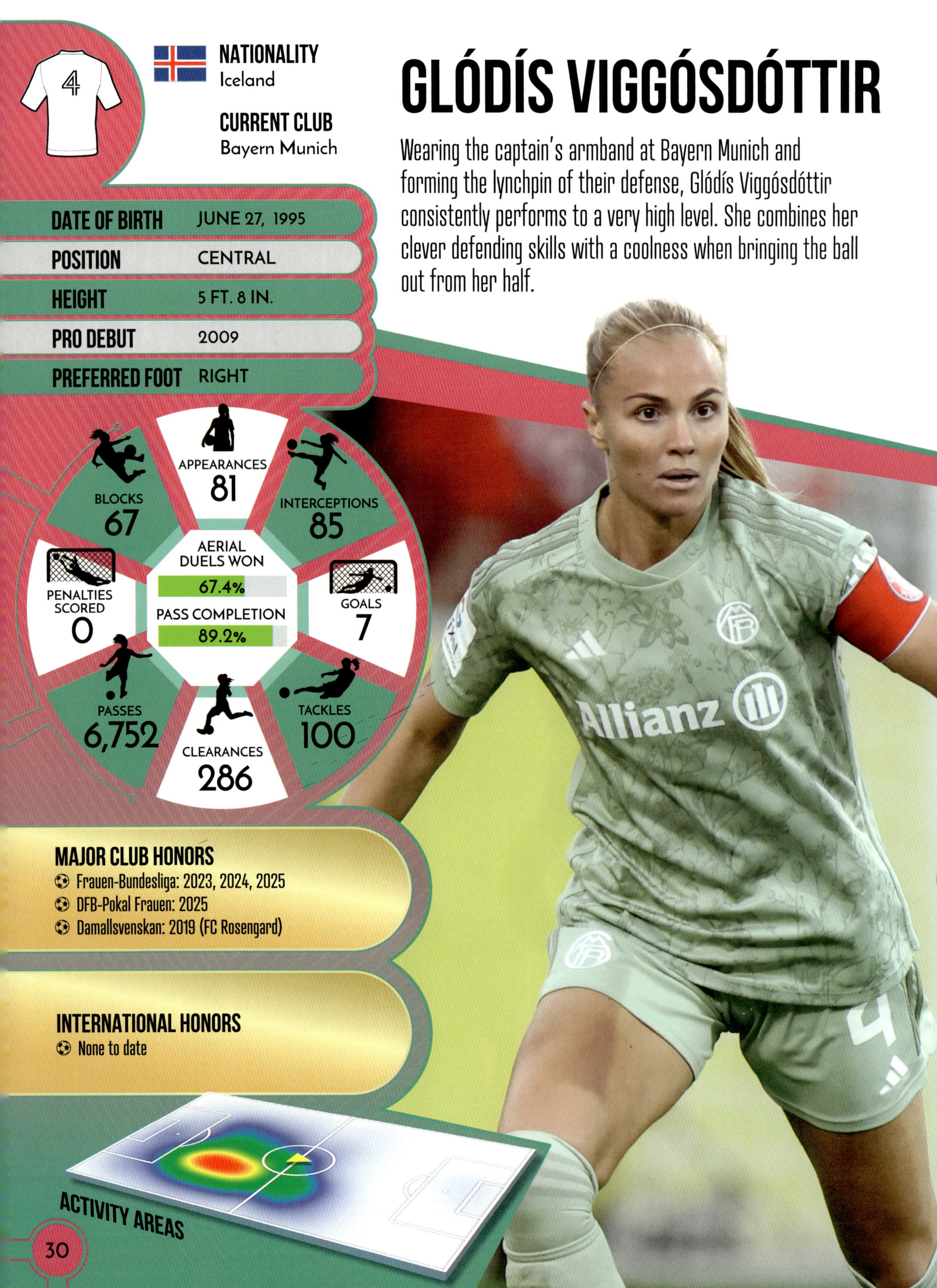

GLÓDÍS VIGGÓSDÓTTIR

Wearing the captain's armband at Bayern Munich and forming the lynchpin of their defense, Glódís Viggósdóttir consistently performs to a very high level. She combines her clever defending skills with a coolness when bringing the ball out from her half.

4

NATIONALITY
Iceland

CURRENT CLUB
Bayern Munich

DATE OF BIRTH	JUNE 27, 1995
POSITION	CENTRAL
HEIGHT	5 FT. 8 IN.
PRO DEBUT	2009
PREFERRED FOOT	RIGHT

APPEARANCES 81
INTERCEPTIONS 85
GOALS 7
TACKLES 100
CLEARANCES 286
PASSES 6,752
PENALTIES SCORED 0
BLOCKS 67

AERIAL DUELS WON 67.4%
PASS COMPLETION 89.2%

MAJOR CLUB HONORS
- Frauen-Bundesliga: 2023, 2024, 2025
- DFB-Pokal Frauen: 2025
- Damallsvenskan: 2019 (FC Rosengard)

INTERNATIONAL HONORS
- None to date

ACTIVITY AREAS

LEAH WILLIAMSON

Leah Williamson has an impressive soccer-playing brain. She can sense danger and get into the best positions to deal with even the smartest forwards. What's more, with the athleticism to reach the ball first, she can build play intelligently from defense.

NATIONALITY
England

CURRENT CLUB
Arsenal

DATE OF BIRTH	JUN 29, 1997
POSITION	CENTRAL
HEIGHT	5 FT. 7 IN.
PRO DEBUT	2014
PREFERRED FOOT	RIGHT

APPEARANCES 55

INTERCEPTIONS 58

GOALS 3

TACKLES 65

CLEARANCES 126

PASSES 4,018

PENALTIES SCORED 0

BLOCKS 19

AERIAL DUELS WON 55.9%

PASS COMPLETION 84.2%

MAJOR CLUB HONORS

⚽ Women's Super League: 2019 ⚽ UEFA Women's Champions League: 2025 ⚽ Women's FA Cup: 2014, 2016 ⚽ Women's FA League Cup: 2015, 2018, 2023, 2024

INTERNATIONAL HONORS

⚽ UEFA Women's Championship: 2022
⚽ Women's Finalissima: 2023

ACTIVITY AREAS

MIDFIELDERS

Whether defensive, playmaker, or operating just behind the forwards, midfielders are crucial to their team's success. A midfielder needs to be technically sound, a quick thinker, and have the fitness to cover big distances during a game. Defensive midfielders protect their back line with strength and timely interceptions. Playmakers are more attack minded and have the job of creating scoring chances. Midfielders can even play close to the strikers in a role that's difficult for the opposition to track and pick up.

WHAT DO THE STATS MEAN?

ASSISTS

A pass, cross, or header to a teammate who then scores counts as an assist. This stat also includes a deflected shot that is converted by a teammate.

SHOTS

Any deliberate strike on goal counts as a shot. The strike does not have to be on target or force a save from the keeper.

CHANCES CREATED

Any pass that results in a shot at goal (whether or not the goal is scored) is regarded as a chance created.

TACKLES

This is the number of times the player has challenged and dispossessed the opposition without committing a foul.

DRIBBLES

This is the number of times the player has gone past an opponent while running with the ball.

SUCCESSFUL PASSES

This shows, as a percentage, how successful the midfielder is at finding teammates with passes.

Did you know?

At the 2023 FIFA Women's World Cup, the top midfielders each covered more than 48 miles (77 kilometers) in total during their tournament appearances.

NATIONALITY
Spain

CURRENT CLUB
Barcelona

AITANA BONMATÍ

With stacks of club and personal prizes, Aitana Bonmatí can score and create from even the slightest of chances. She has exquisite close control, is a dazzling dribbler and famed for delivering pinpoint crosses. She can be a real game changer in the big games.

DATE OF BIRTH	JAN 18, 1998
POSITION	ATTACKING
HEIGHT	5 FT. 4 IN.
PRO DEBUT	2014
PREFERRED FOOT	RIGHT

MAJOR CLUB HONORS

⚽ Liga F: 2020, 2021, 2022, 2023, 2024, 2025
⚽ UEFA Women's Champions League: 2021, 2023, 2024, runner-up 2025 ⚽ Copa de la Reina: 2017, 2018, 2020, 2021, 2022, 2024, 2025

INTERNATIONAL HONORS

⚽ FIFA Women's World Cup: 2023
⚽ UEFA Women's Nations League: 2024

ACTIVITY AREAS

DELPHINE CASCARINO

In an attacking right-sided role, few players can match the speed, skill, and end product of Delphine Cascarino. She has the tricks and flicks to beat defenders and will find a team-mate with a bending cross or a slick through-pass. She is a very capable scorer as well.

NATIONALITY
France

CURRENT CLUB
San Diego Wave

DATE OF BIRTH	FEB 05, 1997
POSITION	WINGER
HEIGHT	5 FT. 5 IN.
PRO DEBUT	2015
PREFERRED FOOT	RIGHT

APPEARANCES	55
DRIBBLES	219
GOALS	13
TACKLES	77
CHANCES CREATED	83
SHOTS	90
PENALTIES SCORED	0
ASSISTS	11
PASSES	1,404
SUCCESSFUL PASSES	75.9%

MAJOR CLUB HONORS

⚽ Première Ligue (Division 1 Féminine): 2015–2024 (x9 all Lyon) ⚽ UEFA Women's Champions League: 2016, 2017, 2018, 2019, 2020, 2022, runner-up 2024 (all Lyon) ⚽ Coupe de France Féminine: 2015, 2016, 2017, 2019, 2020, 2023 (all Lyon)

INTERNATIONAL HONORS

⚽ None to date

ACTIVITY AREAS

NATIONALITY
Scotland

CURRENT CLUB
Chelsea

ERIN CUTHBERT

Erin Cuthbert reached 50 goals for Chelsea in 2023. Her scoring rate in tandem with her incredible work rate in midfield means she is a big performer for the club. Versatile and committed in her tackling, the Scotland ace is a box-to-box menace for her opponents.

DATE OF BIRTH	JUL 19, 1998
POSITION	CENTRAL
HEIGHT	5 FT. 3 IN.
PRO DEBUT	2013
PREFERRED FOOT	RIGHT

APPEARANCES 82

DRIBBLES 134

ASSISTS 7

PENALTIES SCORED 0

PASSES 3,186

SUCCESSFUL PASSES 83.9%

GOALS 18

SHOTS 154

CHANCES CREATED 89

TACKLES 233

MAJOR CLUB HONORS
⚽ Women's Super League: 2017, 2018, 2020, 2021, 2022, 2023, 2024, 2025 ⚽ Women's FA Cup: 2018, 2021, 2022, 2023, 2025 ⚽ UEFA Women's Champions League: Runner-up 2021 ⚽ Women's FA League Cup: 2020, 2021, 2025

INTERNATIONAL HONORS
⚽ None to date

ACTIVITY AREAS

DEBINHA

Opponents often double up on Debinha in a bid to contain the skills and forward bursts that make her shine. Whether operating as a central playmaker or drifting wide to unlock the defense in tight games, the Brazil star has that special X factor in her cleats.

NATIONALITY
Brazil

CURRENT CLUB
Kansas City Current

DATE OF BIRTH	OCT 20, 1991
POSITION	ATTACKING
HEIGHT	5 FT. 2 IN.
PRO DEBUT	2006
PREFERRED FOOT	RIGHT

MAJOR CLUB HONORS

- NWSL Championship: 2018, 2019 (all North Carolina Courage)
- NWSL Shield: 2017, 2018, 2019 (all North Carolina Courage)
- NWSL Challenge Cup: 2022 (North Carolina Courage)

INTERNATIONAL HONORS

- Copa América Femenina: 2018, 2022

ACTIVITY AREAS

NATIONALITY
Haiti

CURRENT CLUB
Lyon

MELCHIE DUMORNAY

Melchie Dumornay shines as an adaptable and attacking midfielder who can pop passes and make unchecked runs into the penalty box. In last year's Women's Champions League she scored four goals and made two assists in her first seven games to underline her value as an attacking force.

DATE OF BIRTH	AUG 17, 2003
POSITION	ATTACKING
HEIGHT	5 FT. 3 IN.
PRO DEBUT	2018
PREFERRED FOOT	RIGHT

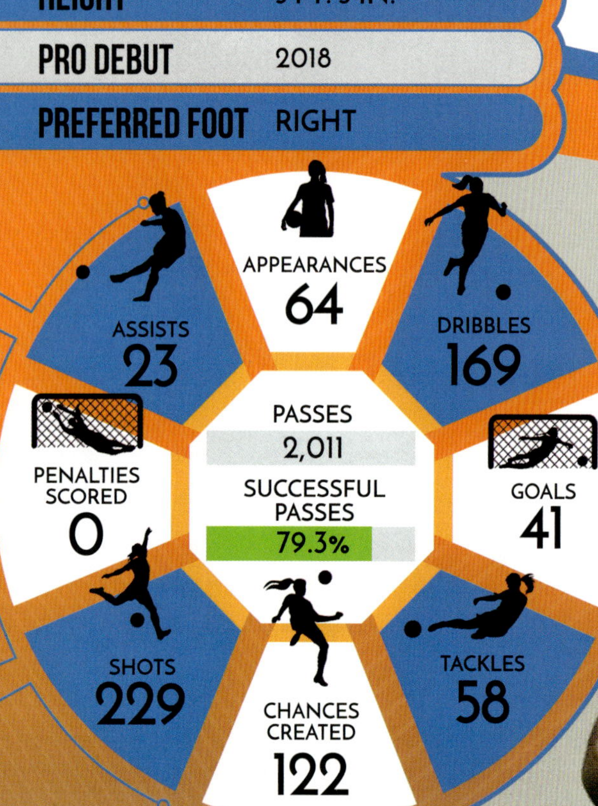

MAJOR CLUB HONORS
- Première Ligue (Division 1 Féminine): 2024, 2025

INTERNATIONAL HONORS
- None to date

ACTIVITY AREAS

GRACE GEYORO

The Paris Saint-Germain star keeps her team ticking between the boxes. Pouncing on mistakes and able to build counter-attacks with one sweeping pass or surging run, Grace Geyoro revels as a gamechanger in midfield. She is an excellent header of the ball as well.

NATIONALITY
France

CURRENT CLUB
Paris Saint-Germain

DATE OF BIRTH	JUL 02, 1997
POSITION	CENTRAL
HEIGHT	5 FT. 6 IN.
PRO DEBUT	2014
PREFERRED FOOT	RIGHT

MAJOR CLUB HONORS
- Division 1 Féminine: 2021
- Coupe de France Féminine: 2018, 2022, 2024
- UEFA Women's Champions League: Runner-up 2015, 2017

INTERNATIONAL HONORS
- None to date

ACTIVITY AREAS

PATRI GUIJARRO

Patri Guijarro sits deep in midfield, ready to break up attacks and set her team forward. Extremely tidy in challenges, she has a right foot that delivers perfect passes and her long-range shooting technique is among the very best.

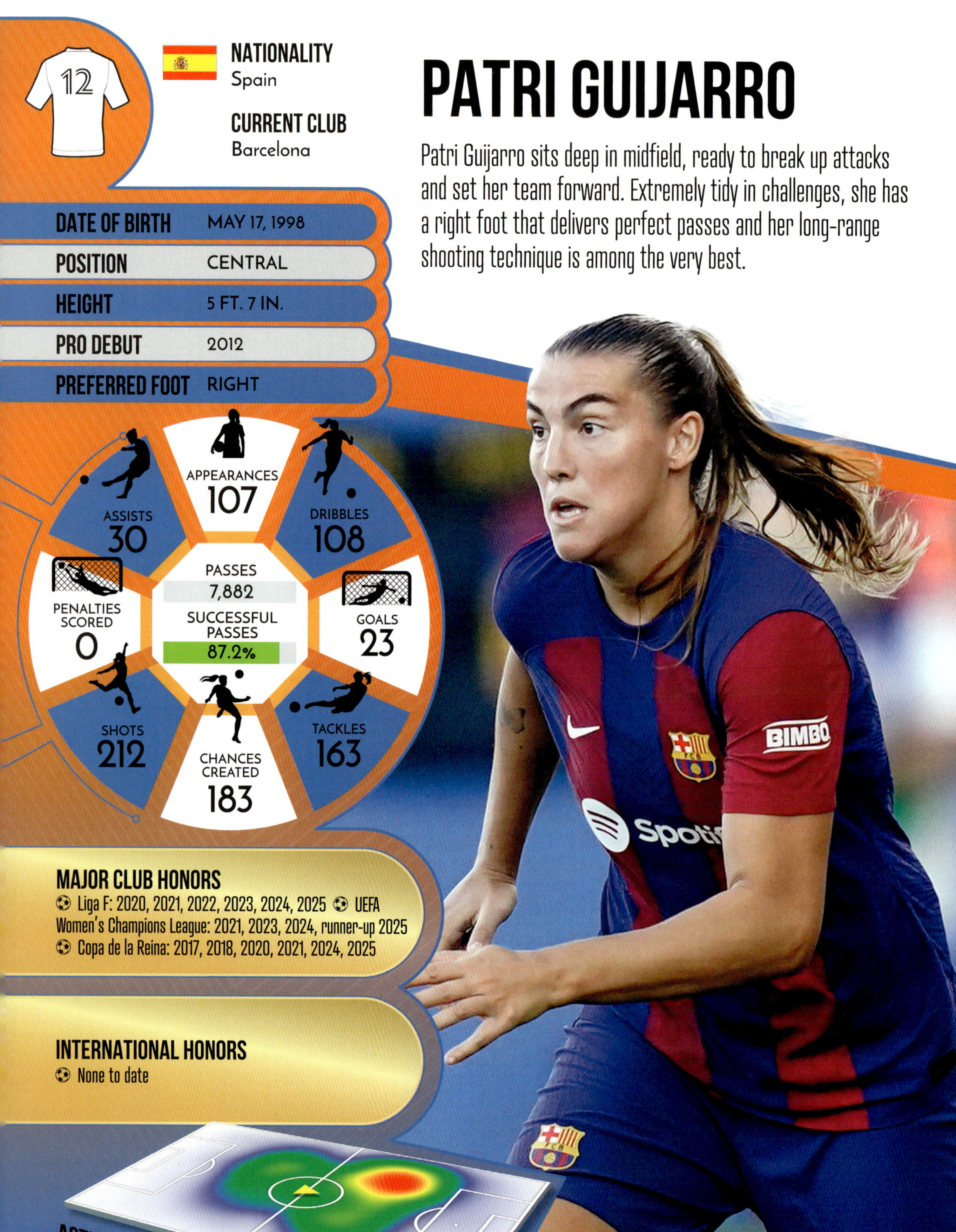

MAJOR CLUB HONORS

⚽ Liga F: 2020, 2021, 2022, 2023, 2024, 2025 ⚽ UEFA Women's Champions League: 2021, 2023, 2024, runner-up 2025 ⚽ Copa de la Reina: 2017, 2018, 2020, 2021, 2024, 2025

INTERNATIONAL HONORS

⚽ None to date

YUI HASEGAWA

The tenacious Yui Hasegawa has a natural ability to protect her defense and win possession in central areas. She combines her tackling skills with an instinct to set up attacks, so don't be surprised to see Hasegawa carry the ball forward and dribble through the lines.

NATIONALITY
Japan

CURRENT CLUB
Manchester City

DATE OF BIRTH	JAN 29, 1997
POSITION	DEFENSIVE
HEIGHT	5 FT. 2 IN.
PRO DEBUT	2013
PREFERRED FOOT	RIGHT

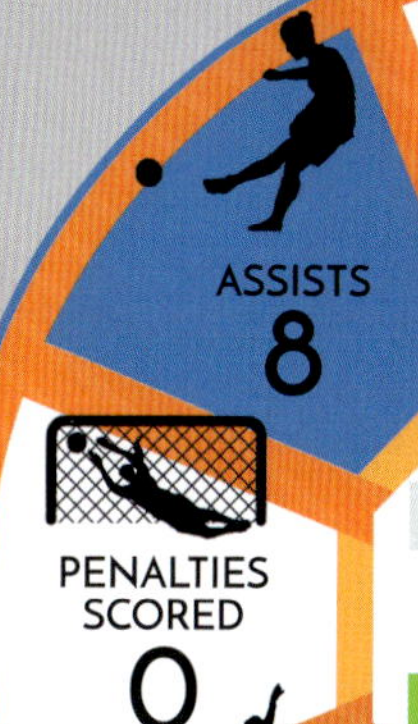

APPEARANCES	72
DRIBBLES	123
GOALS	1
TACKLES	147
CHANCES CREATED	75
SHOTS	39
PENALTIES SCORED	0
ASSISTS	8
PASSES	4,294
SUCCESSFUL PASSES	89.1%

MAJOR CLUB HONORS

- Nadeshiko League: 2015, 2016, 2017, 2018, 2019 (all Tokyo Verdy Beleza)

INTERNATIONAL HONORS

- AFC Women's Asian Cup: 2018

ACTIVITY AREAS

LINDSEY HEAPS

Lindsey Heaps (née Horan) is a creative force in midfield capable of breaking through the back line and getting into forward positions. While she thrives on hitting the net herself, she often takes a split second to scan the field for the best option ahead of her. She loves making late runs into the area.

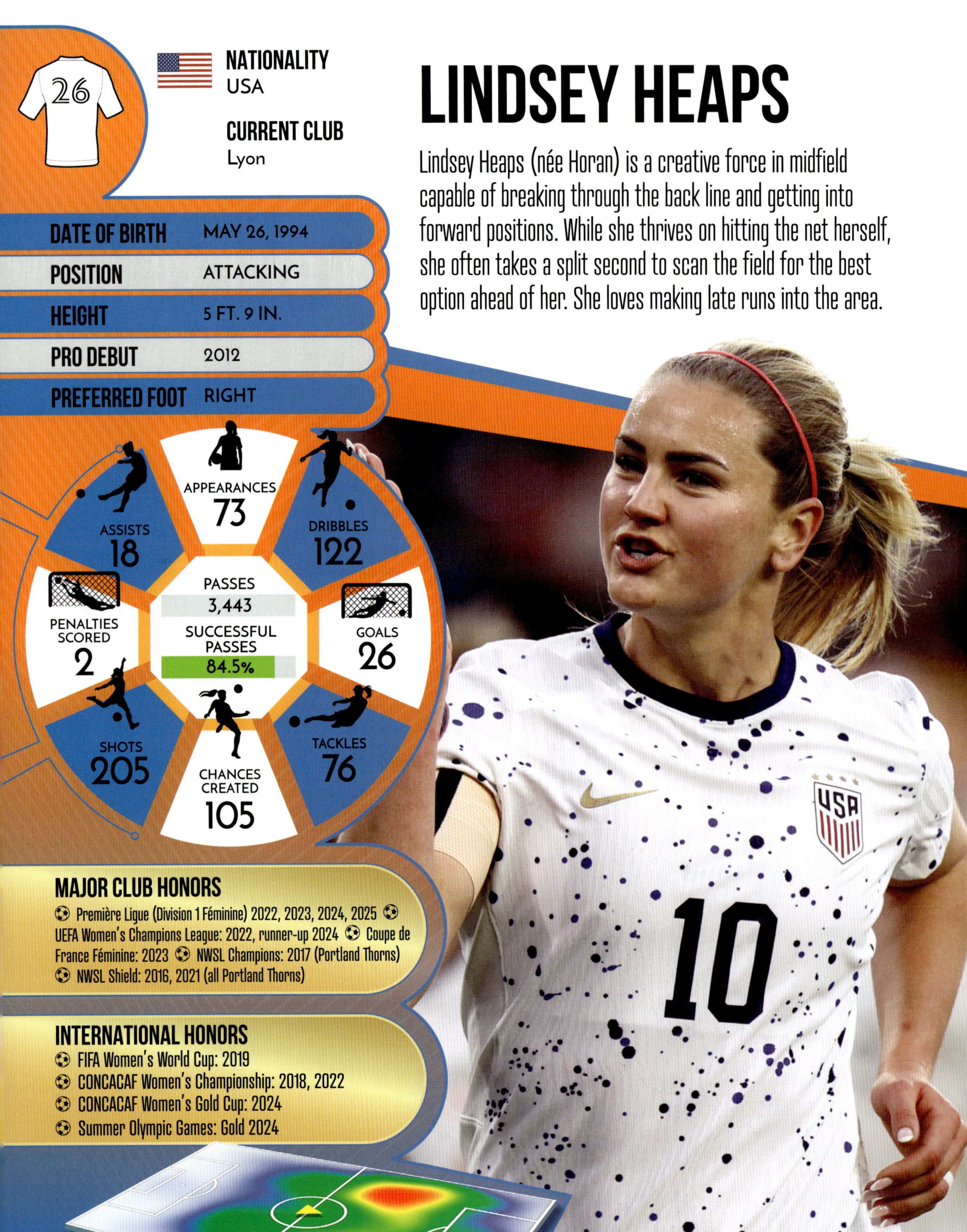

MAJOR CLUB HONORS

⚽ Première Ligue (Division 1 Féminine) 2022, 2023, 2024, 2025 ⚽ UEFA Women's Champions League: 2022, runner-up 2024 ⚽ Coupe de France Féminine: 2023 ⚽ NWSL Champions: 2017 (Portland Thorns) ⚽ NWSL Shield: 2016, 2021 (all Portland Thorns)

INTERNATIONAL HONORS

- ⚽ FIFA Women's World Cup: 2019
- ⚽ CONCACAF Women's Championship: 2018, 2022
- ⚽ CONCACAF Women's Gold Cup: 2024
- ⚽ Summer Olympic Games: Gold 2024

LAUREN HEMP

Playing on the left wing, Lauren Hemp is a nightmare for full-backs to defend against. She dashes forward at every opportunity and has the quick feet to sail past defenders and put a telling pass into the box. She has the courage and physique to outmuscle opponents.

NATIONALITY
England

CURRENT CLUB
Manchester City

DATE OF BIRTH	AUG 07, 2000
POSITION	WINGER
HEIGHT	5 FT. 5 IN.
PRO DEBUT	2016
PREFERRED FOOT	LEFT

MAJOR CLUB HONORS
- Women's FA Cup: 2019
- Women's FA League Cup 2022

MAJOR CLUB HONORS
- Women's FA Cup: 2019
- Women's FA League Cup 2022

ACTIVITY AREAS

NATIONALITY
Scotland

CURRENT CLUB
Arsenal

KIM LITTLE

A model of consistency both in her performances and the desire to win, Kim Little celebrated 350 appearances for Arsenal in 2024, and she's still going strong. A gritty and creative midfielder, Little possesses a sweet right foot and is ice-cool from the penalty spot.

DATE OF BIRTH	JUN 29, 1990
POSITION	CENTRAL
HEIGHT	5 FT. 4 IN.
PRO DEBUT	2006
PREFERRED FOOT	RIGHT

APPEARANCES 69
DRIBBLES 90
GOALS 7
TACKLES 84
CHANCES CREATED 76
SHOTS 50
PENALTIES SCORED 5
ASSISTS 10
PASSES 3,177
SUCCESSFUL PASSES 89.1%

MAJOR CLUB HONORS
⚽ WSL: 2011, 2012, 2019 ⚽ Women's FA Cup: 2009, 2011, 2013 ⚽ UEFA Women's Champions League: 2025 ⚽ Women's FA League Cup: 2011, 2012, 2013, 2018, 2023, 2024 ⚽ NWSL Shield: 2014, 2015 (all Seattle Reign) ⚽ A-League Champions: 2016 (Melbourne City) ⚽ A-League Premiership: 2016 (Melbourne City)

INTERNATIONAL HONORS
⚽ None to date

ACTIVITY AREAS

VICKY LÓPEZ

The skill, maturit,y and finishing ability of this teenager are frightening. When attacking Vicky López has the power and athleticism to skip past defenders and line up a shot. Besides her talent in front of goal, her link-up play and pressing are top class.

NATIONALITY
Spain

CURRENT CLUB
Barcelona

DATE OF BIRTH	JUN 26, 2006
POSITION	ATTACKING
HEIGHT	5 FT. 3 IN.
PRO DEBUT	2021
PREFERRED FOOT	RIGHT

APPEARANCES 75
DRIBBLES 154
GOALS 22
TACKLES 61
CHANCES CREATED 73
SHOTS 147
PENALTIES SCORED 0
ASSISTS 6
PASSES 2,121
SUCCESSFUL PASSES 84.5%

MAJOR CLUB HONORS
- Liga F: 2023, 2024, 2025
- UEFA Women's Champions League: 2023, 2024, runner-up 2025
- Copa de la Reina: 2024, 2025

INTERNATIONAL HONORS
- UEFA Women's Nations League: 2024

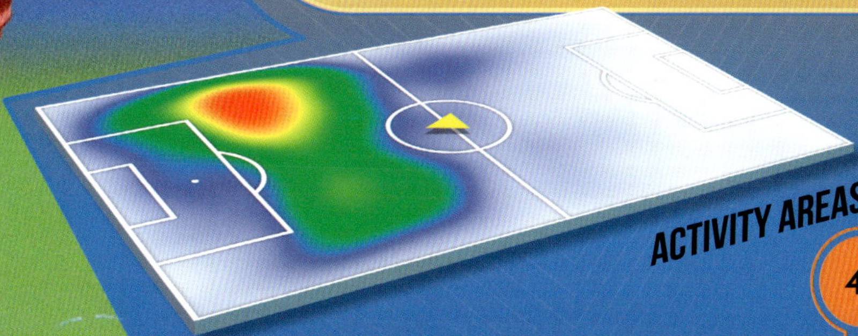

ACTIVITY AREAS

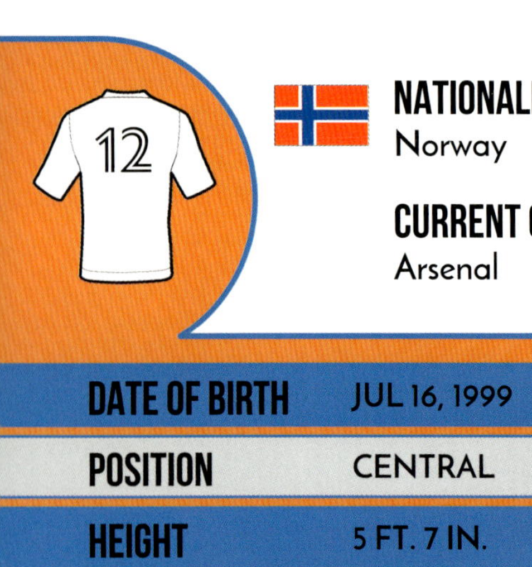

NATIONALITY
Norway

CURRENT CLUB
Arsenal

FRIDA MAANUM

Expect to see Frida Maanum driving her team forward, from deep midfield or a more attacking position. Her sharp footwork helps her wriggle free from challenges and she is not afraid to shoot from distance. She is one of the finest free-kick takers in the WSL.

DATE OF BIRTH	JUL 16, 1999
POSITION	CENTRAL
HEIGHT	5 FT. 7 IN.
PRO DEBUT	2014
PREFERRED FOOT	RIGHT

APPEARANCES 86
DRIBBLES 133
GOALS 26
TACKLES 57
CHANCES CREATED 105
SHOTS 209
PENALTIES SCORED 0
ASSISTS 11
PASSES 2,036
SUCCESSFUL PASSES 80.0%

MAJOR CLUB HONORS
- FA Women's League Cup: 2023, 2024
- UEFA Women's Champions League: 2025

INTERNATIONAL HONORS
- None to date

ACTIVITY AREAS

HINATA MIYAZAWA

With her pace and cool finishing, Hinata Miyazawa does a superb job of supporting the forwards and increasing her team's attacking options. Adept with either foot, she weaves clever passes and cracks shots off with ease. She was the top scorer at the 2023 World Cup.

NATIONALITY
Japan

CURRENT CLUB
Manchester United

20

DATE OF BIRTH	NOV 28, 1999
POSITION	ATTACKING
HEIGHT	5. FT 5 IN.
PRO DEBUT	2018
PREFERRED FOOT	RIGHT

APPEARANCES 31

DRIBBLES 18

GOALS 2

TACKLES 48

CHANCES CREATED 20

SHOTS 36

PENALTIES SCORED 0

ASSISTS 3

PASSES 751

SUCCESSFUL PASSES 84.3%

MAJOR CLUB HONORS

- AFC Women's Club Championship: 2019 (Tokyo Verdy Beleza)
- Women's FA Cup: 2024

INTERNATIONAL HONORS

- None to date

ACTIVITY AREAS

SJOEKE NÜSKEN

A key player for a top club and international team, Nüsken is world class! Strong and athletic, she glides from box to box, dominating the midfield with her tidy tackling coupled with high-quality short and long-range passing.

MAJOR CLUB HONORS

- Women's Super League: 2024, 2025
- Women's FA Cup: 2025
- FA Women's League Cup: 2025

INTERNATIONAL HONORS

- UEFA Nations League: Third place 2024
- Summer Olympic Games: Bronze 2024

LENA OBERDORF

NATIONALITY
Germany

CURRENT CLUB
Bayern Munich

Hailed as one of the best young defensive midfielders in Europe, Lena Oberdorf was snapped up by Bayern Munich in 2024, though a cruciate injury prevented her from making her debut in '24/25. A natural leader, she enjoys pressing and tackling, as well as powering forward when space opens up.

DATE OF BIRTH	DEC 19, 2001
POSITION	DEFENSIVE
HEIGHT	5 FT. 9 IN.
PRO DEBUT	2018
PREFERRED FOOT	RIGHT

APPEARANCES 42
ASSISTS 5
DRIBBLES 47
PASSES 1,631
SUCCESSFUL PASSES 71.5%
PENALTIES SCORED 0
GOALS 8
SHOTS 49
TACKLES 144
CHANCES CREATED 34

MAJOR CLUB HONORS

- Frauen-Bundesliga: 2022 (VfL Wolfsburg),
- UEFA Champions League: Runner-up 2023 (vfL Wolfsburg)
- DFB-Pokal Frauen: 2021, 2022, 2023, 2024 (all vfL Wolfsburg)

INTERNATIONAL HONORS

- UEFA Women's Championship: Runner-up 2022
- UEFA Nations League: Third place 2024

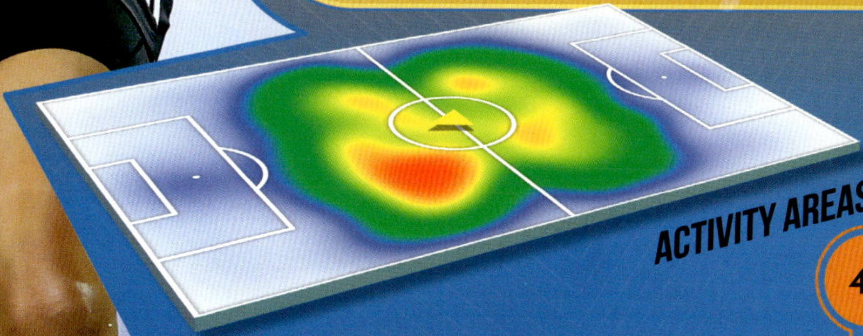

ACTIVITY AREAS

NATIONALITY
Spain

CURRENT CLUB
Barcelona

CLÀUDIA PINA

Able to operate as a midfielder or forward, Barcelona's dangerous number nine has unique attributes that make her a world-class player. Clàudia Pina appears in pockets of space as she probes and passes toward goal, bamboozling even the most disciplined defenses.

DATE OF BIRTH	AUG 12, 2001
POSITION	ATTACKING
HEIGHT	5 FT. 3 IN.
PRO DEBUT	2016
PREFERRED FOOT	RIGHT

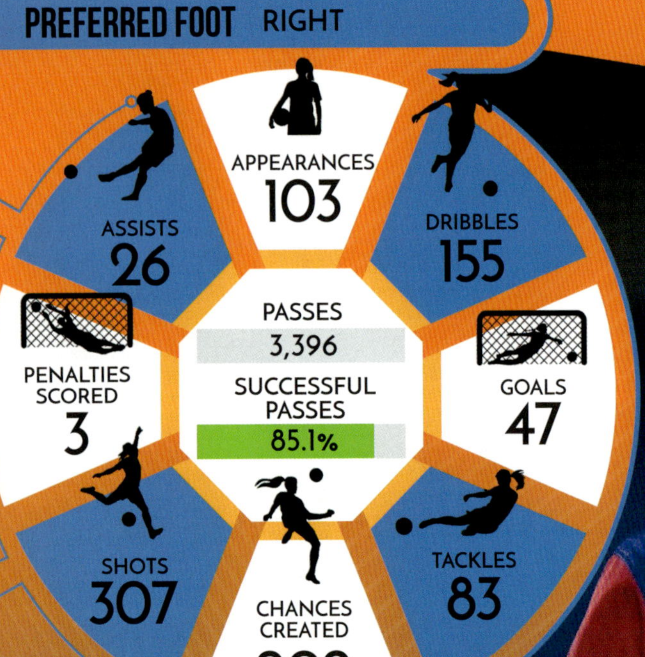

MAJOR CLUB HONORS
- Liga F: 2020, 2022, 2023, 2024, 2025
- UEFA Champions League: 2023, 2024, runner-up 2025
- Copa de la Reina: 2020, 2022, 2024, 2025

INTERNATIONAL HONORS
- None to date

ACTIVITY AREAS

ALEXIA PUTELLAS

Barcelona's decorated captain is a key player for both club and country. Her positional play and attacking instincts are matched by her high-octane defensive work. Alexia Putellas makes ghosting beyond an opponent and hitting a raking pass look so simple.

NATIONALITY
Spain

CURRENT CLUB
Barcelona

DATE OF BIRTH	FEB 04, 1994
POSITION	ATTACKING
HEIGHT	5 FT. 8 IN.
PRO DEBUT	2008
PREFERRED FOOT	LEFT

APPEARANCES 65

DRIBBLES 109

GOALS 31

TACKLES 60

CHANCES CREATED 137

SHOTS 164

PENALTIES SCORED 7

ASSISTS 20

PASSES 2,829

SUCCESSFUL PASSES 83.8%

MAJOR CLUB HONORS

⚽ Liga F: 2013, 2014, 2015, 2020, 2021, 2022, 2023, 2024, 2025 ⚽ UEFA Women's Champions League: 2021, 2023, 2024, runner-up 2025 ⚽ Copa de la Reina: 2013, 2014, 2017, 2018, 2020, 2021, 2022, 2024, 2025

INTERNATIONAL HONORS

⚽ FIFA Women's World Cup: 2023
⚽ UEFA Women's Nations League: 2024

ACTIVITY AREAS

GURO REITEN

Some wingers drift out of games as they wait for the ball. Not Guro Reiten. The left-footed Chelsea favorite enjoys winning possession and advancing forward or leaving opponents dazed with one instinctive flick to a teammate.

MAJOR CLUB HONORS

⚽ Women's Super League: 2020, 2021, 2022, 2023, 2024, 2025 ⚽ UEFA Women's Champions League: Runner-up 2021 ⚽ Women's FA Cup: 2021, 2022, 2023, 2025 ⚽ Women's FA League Cup: 2020, 2021, 2025

INTERNATIONAL HONORS

⚽ None to date

ACTIVITY AREAS

GEORGIA STANWAY

Georgia Stanway's influence may go unnoticed in central midfield but do not underestimate her importance. In transitions, her ability to win second balls and fly into tackles can be the difference between victory and defeat. She is hugely competitive with a strong will to win.

NATIONALITY
England

CURRENT CLUB
Bayern Munich

DATE OF BIRTH	JAN 03, 1999
POSITION	CENTRAL
HEIGHT	5 FT. 5 IN.
PRO DEBUT	2015
PREFERRED FOOT	RIGHT

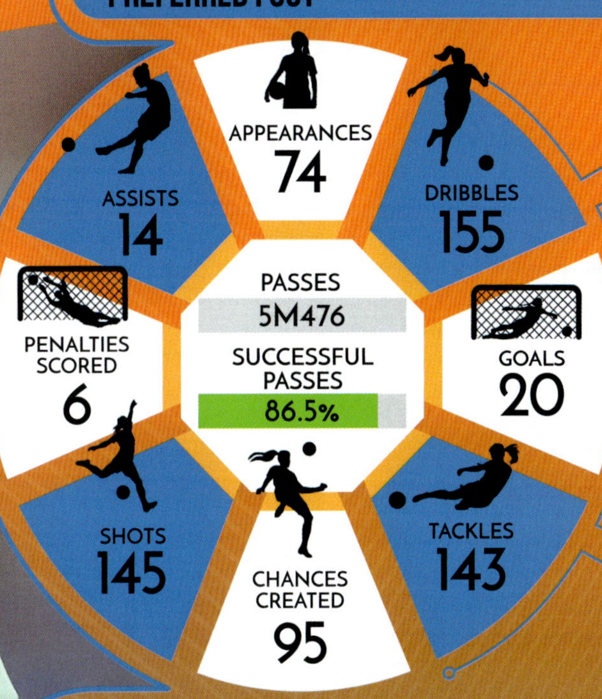

MAJOR CLUB HONORS

⚽ Frauen-Bundesliga: 2023, 2024, 2025 ⚽ Women's Super League: 2016 (Manchester City) ⚽ Women's FA Cup: 2017, 2019, 2020 (Manchester City) ⚽ Women's FA League Cup: 2016, 2019, 2022 (Manchester City)

INTERNATIONAL HONORS

⚽ UEFA Women's Championship: 2022
⚽ FIFA Women's World Cup: Runner-up 2023
⚽ Women's Finalissima: 2023

ACTIVITY AREAS

NATIONALITY
England

CURRENT CLUB
Manchester United

ELLA TOONE

Goals, assists, and world-class performances are what Ella Toone has in her locker. An intelligent midfielder who sits off the forwards, she makes telling contributions with her energy, technique, and visionary passing. "Tooney" can lift her teammates and the crowd with one magic moment.

DATE OF BIRTH	SEP 02, 1999
POSITION	CENTRAL
HEIGHT	5 FT. 3 IN.
PRO DEBUT	2015
PREFERRED FOOT	RIGHT

APPEARANCES 62

DRIBBLES 88

GOALS 14

TACKLES 50

CHANCES CREATED 95

SHOTS 111

PENALTIES SCORED 0

ASSISTS 14

PASSES 2,424

SUCCESSFUL PASSES 79.7%

MAJOR CLUB HONORS

- Women's Super League: 2016 (Manchester City)
- FA Women's Championship: 2019
- Women's FA Cup: 2024
- Women's FA League Cup: 2016 (Manchester City)

INTERNATIONAL HONORS

- UEFA Women's Championship: 2022
- Women's Finalissima: 2023
- FIFA Women's World Cup: Runner-up 2023

ACTIVITY AREAS

DANIËLLE VAN DE DONK

Thanks to her vision and experience, Daniëlle van de Donk creates scoring chances that frequently hurt the opposition. Efficient with her tackling and passing, she loves going forward, ready to fire a right-footed shot. Her heading is another top skill.

NATIONALITY
Netherlands

CURRENT CLUB
Lyon

17

DATE OF BIRTH	AUG 5,1991
POSITION	CENTRAL
HEIGHT	1.60 M
PRO DEBUT	2008
PREFERRED FOOT	RIGHT

APPEARANCES 84

DRIBBLES 104

GOALS 16

TACKLES 98

CHANCES CREATED 93

SHOTS 122

PENALTIES SCORED 0

ASSISTS 11

PASSES 2,450

SUCCESSFUL PASSES 82.0%

MAJOR CLUB HONORS

- Première Ligue (Division 1 Féminine): 2022, 2023, 2024, 2025
- UEFA Women's Champions League: 2022, runner-up 2024
- Women's FA Cup: 2016 (Arsenal)

INTERNATIONAL HONORS

- UEFA Women's Championship: 2017
- FIFA Women's World Cup: Runner-up 2019

ACTIVITY AREAS

NATIONALITY
England

CURRENT CLUB
Chelsea

KEIRA WALSH

Keira Walsh disrupts opponents in central areas and recycles the ball superbly. More than just a defensive player, her forward passes and intelligent movement expand her team's options. Vocal and powerful yet always in control.

DATE OF BIRTH	APR 08, 1997
POSITION	DEFENSIVE
HEIGHT	5 FT. 5 IN.
PRO DEBUT	2014
PREFERRED FOOT	RIGHT

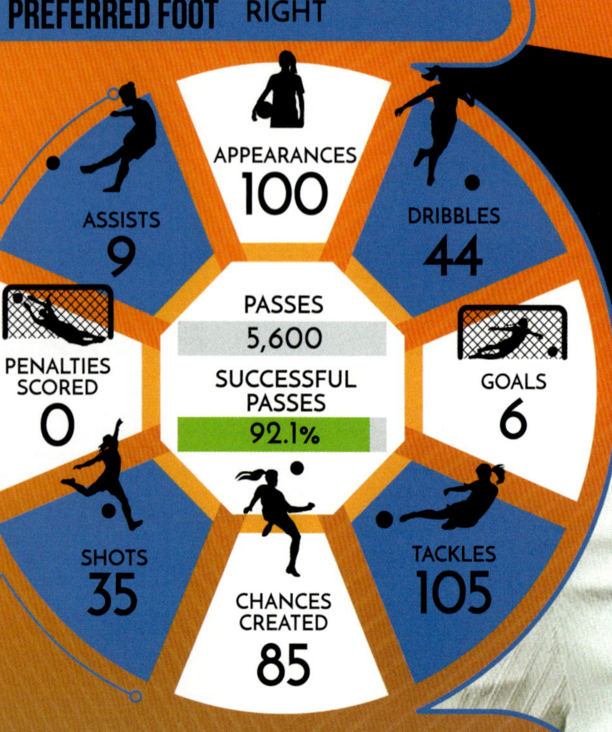

MAJOR CLUB HONORS

⚽ Liga F: 2023, 2024 (all Barça) ⚽ UEFA Champions League: 2023, 2024 (all Barça) ⚽ Women's Super League: 2016 (Man City), 2025 ⚽ Copa de la Reina: 2024 (Barça) ⚽ Women's FA Cup: 2017, 2019, 2020 (all Man City) ⚽ Women's FA League Cup: 2014*, 2016*, 2019*, 2022* (*Man City), 2025

INTERNATIONAL HONORS

- ⚽ UEFA Women's Championship: 2022
- ⚽ Women's Finalissima: 2023
- ⚽ FIFA Women's World Cup: Runner-up 2023

ACTIVITY AREAS

CAROLINE WEIR

Tall, agile, strong, and with a left foot that does special things, Caroline Weir sparkles in her attacking midfield duties. Her coaches love how she shoots and hits the target from long range, plus when she connects beautifully with crosses. She offers the complete package.

NATIONALITY
Scotland

CURRENT CLUB
Real Madrid

DATE OF BIRTH	JUN 20, 1995
POSITION	ATTACKING
HEIGHT	5 FT. 8 IN.
PRO DEBUT	2011
PREFERRED FOOT	LEFT

APPEARANCES 68

ASSISTS 23

DRIBBLES 137

PASSES 2,379

SUCCESSFUL PASSES 85.8

PENALTIES SCORED 2

GOALS 34

SHOTS 186

TACKLES 56

CHANCES CREATED 162

MAJOR CLUB HONORS

⚽ Women's FA Cup: 2014 (Arsenal), 2019,* 2020* (*Manchester City), ⚽ Women's FA League Cup: 2019, 2020 (all Manchester City)

INTERNATIONAL HONORS

⚽ None to date

ACTIVITY AREAS

FORWARDS

These are the players who usually make the most headlines. Also known as strikers, their task is to do the most important thing in soccer — score goals! Forwards need a range of skills to do this, from accurate shooting to brave heading and well-timed runs into the penalty box. These players can be big and strong or small and quick. Sometimes they play in a striking pair or as a trio, or other times they lead the attack on their own. Forwards love being the hero when they hit the back of the net.

WHAT DO THE STATS MEAN?

GOALS

This is the total number of goals a forward has scored. The figure spans across all the top clubs the player has represented in the past three seasons.

ASSISTS

A pass, cross, or header to a teammate who then scores counts as an assist. This stat also includes a deflected shot that is immediately converted by a teammate.

CONVERSION RATE

The percentage shows how good the player is at taking their chance in front of goal. If a player scores two goals from four shots, their conversion rate is 50 percent.

128

MINUTES PER GOAL

This is the average length of time it takes for the player to score. It is calculated across all the minutes the player has played in the past three seasons at top level.

Did you know?

Manchester City's Dutch star Vivianne Miedema has won the Women's Super League golden boot twice in her career and is also the league's all-time top scorer. In seven seasons with Arsenal she hit the net 80 times.

BARBRA BANDA

Barbra Banda took the NWSL by storm in 2024, winning the Championship, Shield, and MVP award in her first season. She is a complete center-forward who can work the channels, use her strength to make assists, or drive through the center to unleash accurate shots.

MAJOR CLUB HONORS

- NWSL Championship: 2024

INTERNATIONAL HONORS

- COSAFA Women's Championship: 2022

STINA BLACKSTENIUS

A key central striker in Arsenal's attacking formation, Stina Blackstenius has the power, skill, and poise to convert chances, especially inside the penalty box. Most notably, she came off the bench to score the winner in the 2024/'25 UEFA Women's Champions League final.

NATIONALITY
Sweden

CURRENT CLUB
Arsenal

DATE OF BIRTH	FEB 05, 1996
POSITION	FORWARD
HEIGHT	5 FT. 8½ IN.
PRO DEBUT	2013
PREFERRED FOOT	RIGHT

GOALS	27
PENALTIES SCORED	0
ASSISTS	6
GOALS RIGHT	19
SHOTS	192
HEADED GOALS	2
HAT TRICKS	0
GOALS LEFT	6
APPEARANCES	81
CONVERSION RATE	14.1%
MINUTES PER GOAL	157

MAJOR CLUB HONORS

- UEFA Women's Champions League: 2025
- Women's FA League Cup: 2023, 2024

INTERNATIONAL HONORS

- Women's World Cup: Third place 2019, 2023
- Summer Summer Olympic Games: Silver 2016, silver 2020 (2021)

ACTIVITY AREAS

NATIONALITY
Spain

CURRENT CLUB
Arsenal

MARIONA CALDENTEY

World Cup winner Mariona Caldentey took little time to open her scoring account after joining Arsenal in 2024. She regularly found the net in her debut season, showcasing her touch and vision around the box, and announcing herself as one of the most versitile attackers in the WSL.

DATE OF BIRTH	MAR 19, 1996
POSITION	FORWARD
HEIGHT	5 FT. 5 IN.
PRO DEBUT	2011
PREFERRED FOOT	RIGHT

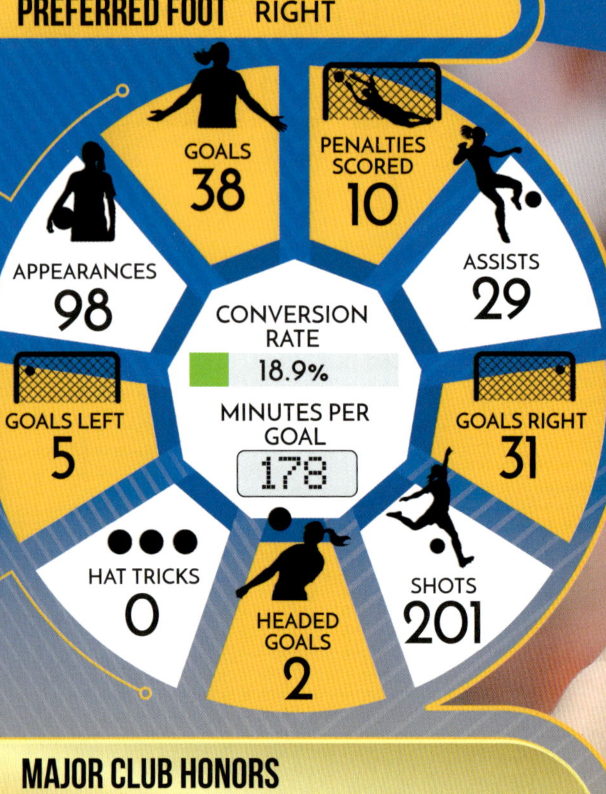

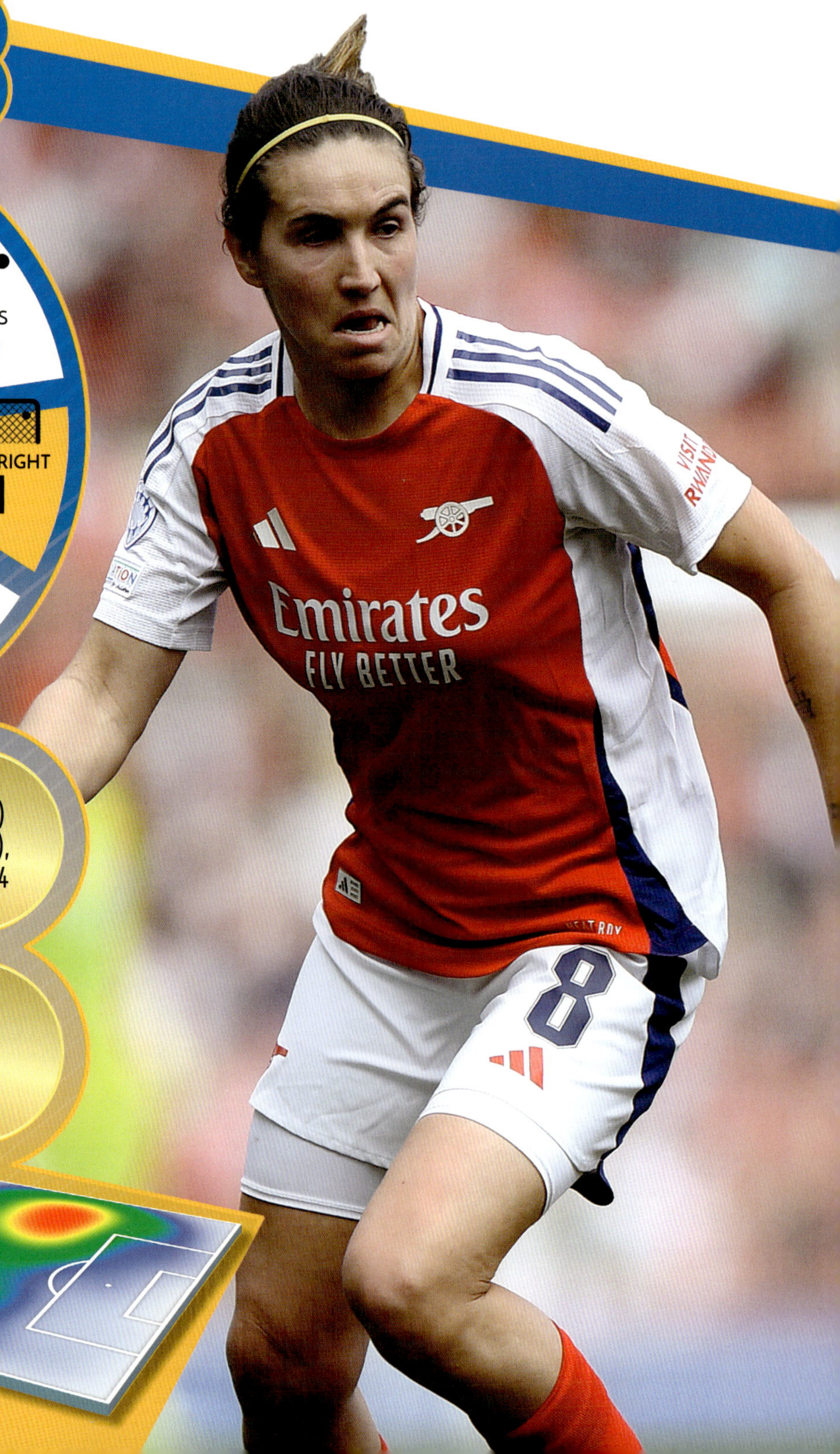

MAJOR CLUB HONORS

- Liga F: 2015, 2020, 2021, 2022, 2023, 2024 (all Barça)
- UEFA Champions League: 2021, 2023, 2024 (all Barça), 2025
- Copa de la Reina: 2017, 2018, 2020, 2021, 2024 (all Barça)

INTERNATIONAL HONORS

- FIFA Women's World Cup: 2023
- UEFA Women's Nations League: 2024

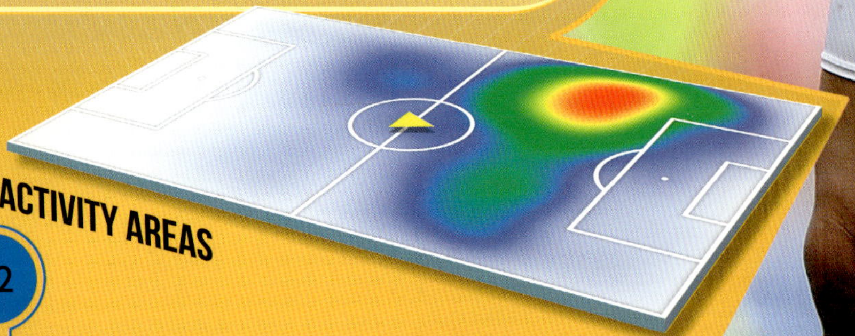

ACTIVITY AREAS

KADIDIATOU DIANI

Kadidiatou Diani is a huge threat in attacking areas. Not only is she clinical inside the box but her dribbling and speed allow her to open up opportunities for her team. As she proved at the 2023 World Cup, where she was the second highest goal scorer, Diani rises for the big occasion.

NATIONALITY
France

CURRENT CLUB
Lyon

DATE OF BIRTH	APR 01, 1995
POSITION	FORWARD
HEIGHT	5 FT. 7 IN.
PRO DEBUT	2011
PREFERRED FOOT	RIGHT

GOALS 52
PENALTIES SCORED 7
ASSISTS 26
APPEARANCES 82
CONVERSION RATE 22.3%
MINUTES PER GOAL 114
GOALS LEFT 5
GOALS RIGHT 35
HAT TRICKS 2
HEADED GOALS 11
SHOTS 233

MAJOR CLUB HONORS
- Première Ligue (Division 1 Féminine): 2021 (PSG), 2024, 2025
- UEFA Champions League: Runner-up 2024
- Coupe de France Féminine: 2018, 2022 (all PSG)

INTERNATIONAL HONORS
- None to date

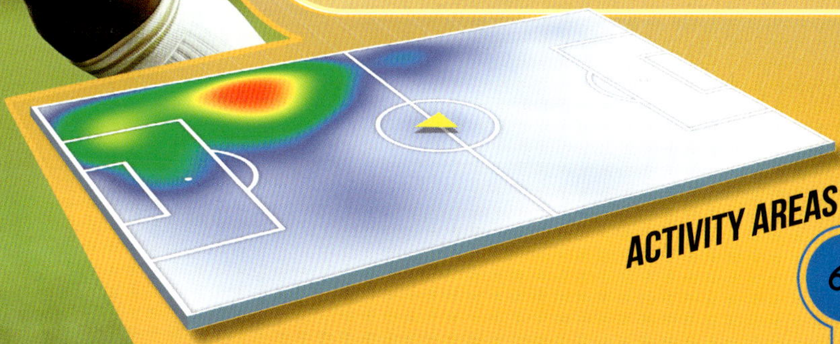

ACTIVITY AREAS

NATIONALITY
Norway

CURRENT CLUB
Barcelona

CAROLINE GRAHAM HANSEN

Caroline Graham Hansen is a natural goal scorer and one of the finest dribblers around, which are two reasons why she has the honor of wearing Barcelona's number 10 shirt. She's known for slaloming past defenders and delivering clever passes and crosses. Graham hasn't even reached her peak yet.

DATE OF BIRTH	FEB 18, 1995
POSITION	FORWARD
HEIGHT	5 FT. 9 IN.
PRO DEBUT	2010
PREFERRED FOOT	RIGHT

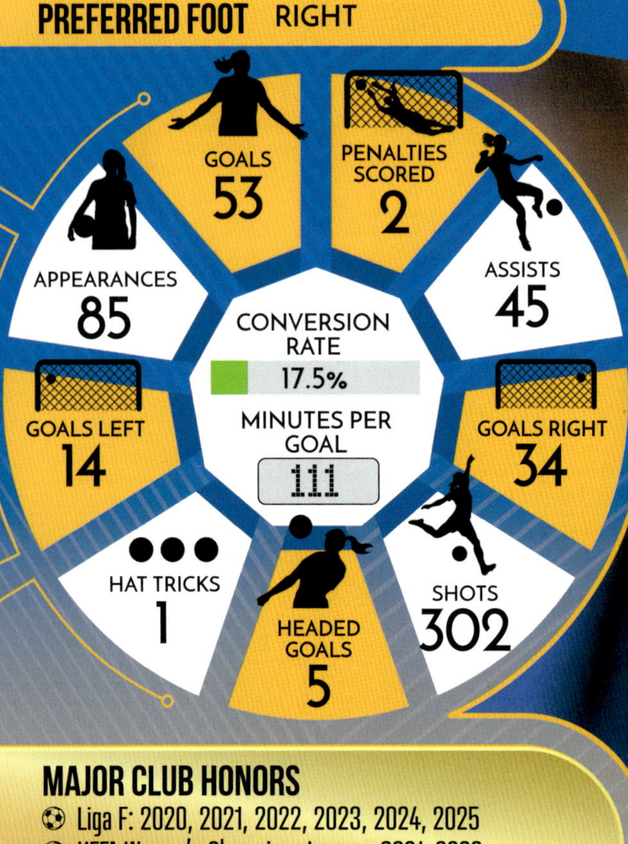

MAJOR CLUB HONORS
⚽ Liga F: 2020, 2021, 2022, 2023, 2024, 2025 ⚽ UEFA Women's Champions League: 2021, 2023, 2024, runner-up 2025 ⚽ Copa de la Reina: 2025 ⚽ Frauen Bundesliga: 2017, 2018, 2019 (all VfL Wolfsburg)

INTERNATIONAL HONORS
⚽ UEFA Women's Championship: Runner-up 2013

ACTIVITY AREAS

PERNILLE HARDER

Able to finish with her right or left foot, Pernille Harder is a slick and versatile attacker. The Denmark captain drives into space with her powerful runs and has the coolness and vision to execute a shot or assist. She is very capable of scoring from free kicks and headers too.

NATIONALITY
Denmark

CURRENT CLUB
Bayern Munich

DATE OF BIRTH	NOV 15, 1992
POSITION	FORWARD
HEIGHT	5 FT. 7 IN.
PRO DEBUT	2007
PREFERRED FOOT	BOTH

GOALS 40
PENALTIES SCORED 1
ASSISTS 14
APPEARANCES 62
CONVERSION RATE 21.7%
MINUTES PER GOAL 114
GOALS LEFT 7
GOALS RIGHT 21
HAT TRICKS 4
HEADED GOALS 12
SHOTS 184

MAJOR CLUB HONORS

⚽ Frauen-Bundesliga: 2017*, '18*, '19*, '20* (*VfL Wolfsburg), 2024, 2025 ⚽ DFB-Pokal Frauen: 2017*, '18*, '19*, '20* (*VfL Wolfsburg), 2025 ⚽ Women's Super League: 2021, 2022, 2023 (all Chelsea) ⚽ Women's FA Cup: 2021, 2022, 2023 (all Chelsea) ⚽ UEFA Women's Champions League: Runner-up 2021 (Chelsea) runner-up 2018*, 2020* (*VfL Wolfsburg)

INTERNATIONAL HONORS

⚽ UEFA Women's Championship: Runner-up 2017

ACTIVITY AREAS

NATIONALITY
Norway

CURRENT CLUB
Lyon

ADA HEGERBERG

Ada Hegerberg has been a world-class player for more than a decade—a testament to both her skills and consistency at the top! As well as winning multiple team trophies, the striker is the leading UEFA Champions League scorer with more than 60 goals, and was the inaugural Ballon d'Or Féminin winner in 2018.

DATE OF BIRTH	JUL 10, 1995
POSITION	STRIKER
HEIGHT	5 FT. 9 IN.
PRO DEBUT	2010
PREFERRED FOOT	RIGHT

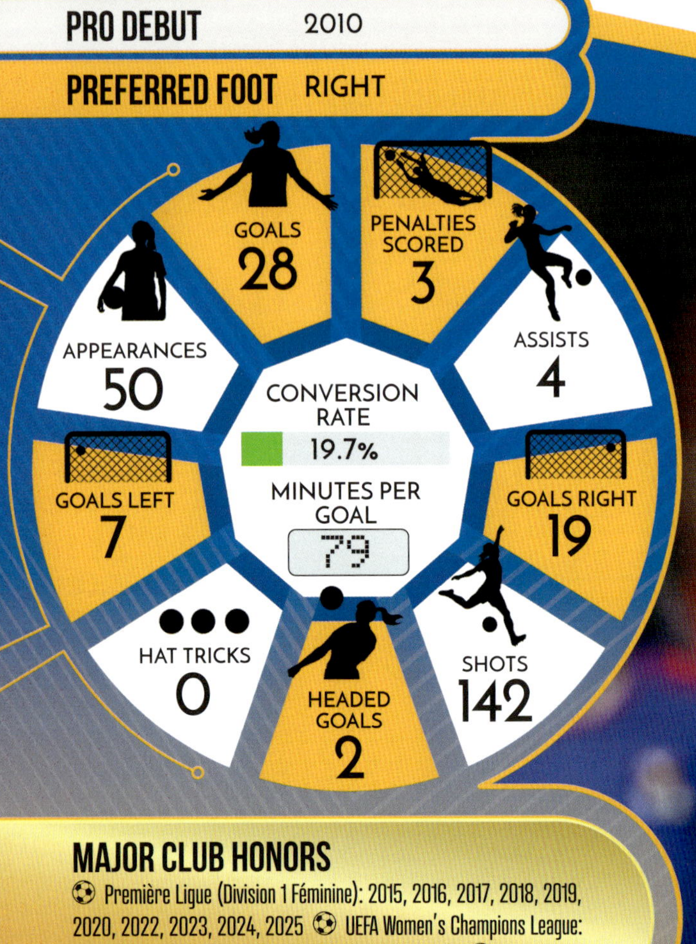

MAJOR CLUB HONORS

⚽ Première Ligue (Division 1 Féminine): 2015, 2016, 2017, 2018, 2019, 2020, 2022, 2023, 2024, 2025 ⚽ UEFA Women's Champions League: 2016, 2017, 2018, 2019, 2020, 2022, runner-up 2024 ⚽ Coupe de France Féminine: 2015, 2016, 2017, 2019, 2020, 2023

INTERNATIONAL HONORS

⚽ UEFA Women's Championship: Runner-up 2013

ACTIVITY AREAS

LAUREN JAMES

One of the breakout stars at the 2023 World Cup, Lauren James is capable of spectacular goals and assists. She often plays in wide positions and cuts inside to shoot or finds a pass with either foot. One of her trademark finishes is to bend the ball inside the far post from range.

NATIONALITY
England

CURRENT CLUB
Chelsea

DATE OF BIRTH	SEP 29, 2001
POSITION	FORWARD
HEIGHT	5 FT. 9 IN.
PRO DEBUT	2017
PREFERRED FOOT	RIGHT

GOALS	24
PENALTIES SCORED	0
ASSISTS	8
GOALS RIGHT	12
SHOTS	174
HEADED GOALS	0
HAT TRICKS	2
GOALS LEFT	12
APPEARANCES	62
CONVERSION RATE	13.8%
MINUTES PER GOAL	170

MAJOR CLUB HONORS
- Women's Super League: 2022, 2023, 2024, 2025
- FA Women's Cup: 2022, 2023, 2025
- FA Women's League Cup: 2025

INTERNATIONAL HONORS
- FIFA Women's World Cup: Runner-up 2023
- FIFA Women's Finalissima: 2023

ACTIVITY AREAS

NATIONALITY
Australia

CURRENT CLUB
Chelsea

SAM KERR

Regarded as one of the best strikers ever, Sam Kerr uses her speed and positional sense to unlock defenses and is clinical in front of goal. She is a spectacular finisher, famous for her volleys, lobs, and long-range rockets. Injury kept her out of action last season but she is back now, ready to thrill fans.

DATE OF BIRTH	SEP 10, 1993
POSITION	STRIKER
HEIGHT	5 FT 6 IN.
PRO DEBUT	2008
PREFERRED FOOT	RIGHT

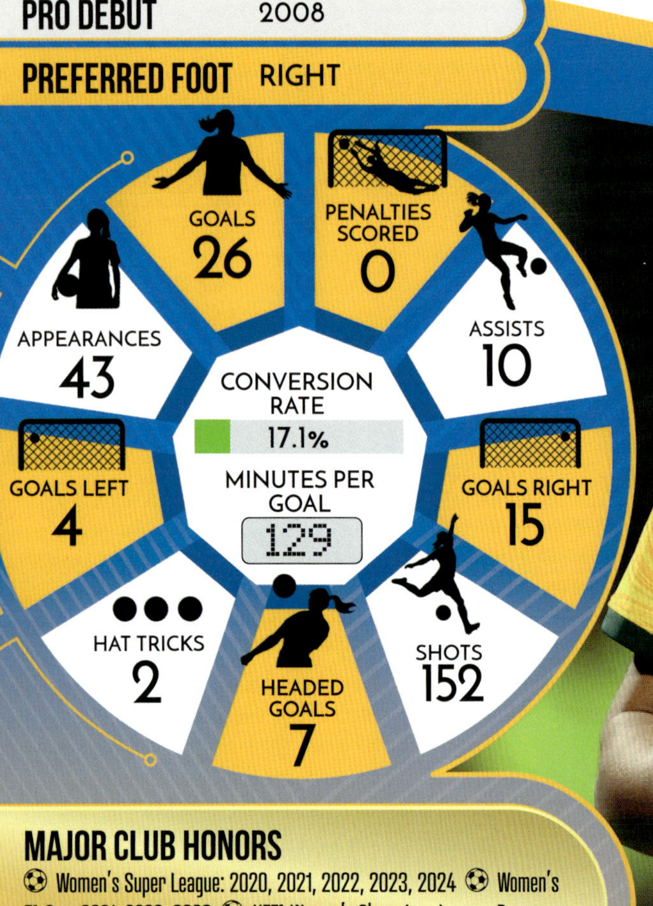

MAJOR CLUB HONORS
⚽ Women's Super League: 2020, 2021, 2022, 2023, 2024 ⚽ Women's FA Cup: 2021, 2022, 2023 ⚽ UEFA Women's Champions League: Runner-up 2021 ⚽ A-League Championship: 2013 (Sydney FC) ⚽ NWSL Shield: 2013 (Western New York Flash) ⚽ A-League Premiership: 2014 (Perth Glory)

INTERNATIONAL HONORS
⚽ AFC Women's Asian Cup: 2010

ACTIVITY AREAS

RACHEAL KUNDANANJI

Joining Bay FC for a record fee of about $800,000 in 2024, Racheal Kundananji is a thrilling forward. She is super confident in possession and spins clear of her marker to connect with crosses and passes. Kundananji's technique and timing inside the box mean she needs only a sniff of a chance to beat a goalkeeper.

NATIONALITY
Zambia

CURRENT CLUB
Bay FC

DATE OF BIRTH	JUN 03, 2000
POSITION	FORWARD
HEIGHT	5 FT.7 IN.
PRO DEBUT	2018
PREFERRED FOOT	RIGHT

GOALS	39
PENALTIES SCORED	0
ASSISTS	11
GOALS RIGHT	21
SHOTS	268
HEADED GOALS	4
HAT TRICKS	2
GOALS LEFT	14
APPEARANCES	75
CONVERSION RATE	14.6%
MINUTES PER GOAL	154

MAJOR CLUB HONORS
- FAZ Women Super League: 2018 (Indeni Roses)
- Kazakhstani Championship: 2019, 2020 (all BIIK Kazygurt)

INTERNATIONAL HONORS
- None to date

ACTIVITY AREAS

NATIONALITY
France

CURRENT CLUB
Lyon

EUGÉNIE LE SOMMER

Eugénie Le Sommer is into the 18th season of a prolific career and remains a potent force in front of goal. The record scorer for France and Lyon, she is so difficult to stop as she powers into the box and blasts, curls, or chips into the net. Le Sommer is an icon of the game.

DATE OF BIRTH	MAY 18, 1989
POSITION	FORWARD
HEIGHT	5 FT. 3 IN.
PRO DEBUT	2007
PREFERRED FOOT	RIGHT

GOALS 28

PENALTIES SCORED 0

ASSISTS 12

APPEARANCES 72

CONVERSION RATE 18.1%

MINUTES PER GOAL 132

GOALS LEFT 11

GOALS RIGHT 12

HAT TRICKS 0

HEADED GOALS 5

SHOTS 155

MAJOR CLUB HONORS

⚽ Première Ligue (Division 1 Féminine): 2011–2020, 2022–2025 ⚽ UEFA Women's Champions League: 2011, 2012, 2016, 2017, 2018, 2019, 2020, 2022, runner-up 2024 ⚽ Coupe de France Féminine: 2012-2017, 2019, 2020, 2023

INTERNATIONAL HONORS

⚽ None to date

ACTIVITY AREAS

BETH MEAD

Beth Mead is a gamechanger in her favored right-sided role. Playing on the shoulder of defenders, she can trap the ball and turn to run into space or chase it in the channels and link up with other attackers. Her 33 goals in her first 63 England games underscores her world-class status.

NATIONALITY
England

CURRENT CLUB
Arsenal

DATE OF BIRTH	MAY 09, 1995
POSITION	FORWARD
HEIGHT	5 FT. 4 IN.
PRO DEBUT	2011
PREFERRED FOOT	RIGHT

GOALS	20
PENALTIES SCORED	0
ASSISTS	3
GOALS RIGHT	12
SHOTS	105
HEADED GOALS	2
HAT TRICKS	0
GOALS LEFT	6
APPEARANCES	60
CONVERSION RATE	19.0%
MINUTES PER GOAL	185

MAJOR CLUB HONORS

- Women's Super League: 2019
- UEFA Women's Champions League: 2025
- Women's FA League Cup: 2018, 2023, 2024

INTERNATIONAL HONORS

- UEFA Women's Championship: 2022

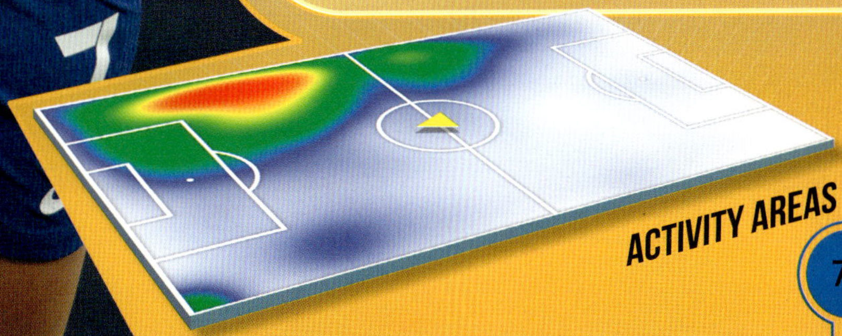

ACTIVITY AREAS

VIVIANNE MIEDEMA

Scorer of a record 100 goals in only 110 games during her time at Arsenal highlights just how ruthless Vivianne Miedema is in front of goal. Tall, physical, and equally skillful on the deck as she is in the air, the Dutch legend has all the tricks and powers required to hurt the opposition.

MAJOR CLUB HONORS

- Women's Super League: 2019 (Arsenal)
- Frauen Bundesliga: 2015, 2016 (Bayern Munich)
- Women's FA League Cup: 2018, 2023, 2024 (Arsenal)

INTERNATIONAL HONORS

- UEFA Women's Championship: 2017
- FIFA Women's World Cup: Runner-up 2019

EWA PAJOR

Poland's most potent female forward, Ewa Pajor scores headers, long-range goals, and accurate tap-ins at a prolific rate. She has been known to run rampant in the European competitions as she bullies defenders and finds space to let fly with her dangerous right foot.

NATIONALITY
Poland

CURRENT CLUB
Barcelona

DATE OF BIRTH	DEC 03, 1996
POSITION	STRIKER
HEIGHT	5 FT. 6 IN.
PRO DEBUT	2012
PREFERRED FOOT	RIGHT

GOALS	71
PENALTIES SCORED	1
ASSISTS	27
GOALS RIGHT	45
SHOTS	334
HEADED GOALS	12
HAT TRICKS	5
GOALS LEFT	14
APPEARANCES	88
CONVERSION RATE	21.3%
MINUTES PER GOAL	89

MAJOR CLUB HONORS

⚽ Frauen-Bundesliga: 2017-20, '22 (all VfL Wolfsburg) ⚽ UEFA Women's Champions League: 2016*, 2018*, 2020*, 2023* (*Vfl Wolfsburg; all as runner-up), runner-up 2025 ⚽ Copa de la Reina: 2025 ⚽ DFB-Pokal Frauen: 2016-2024 (x9 – all Vfl Wolfsburg)

INTERNATIONAL HONORS

⚽ None to date

ACTIVITY AREAS

SALMA PARALLUELO

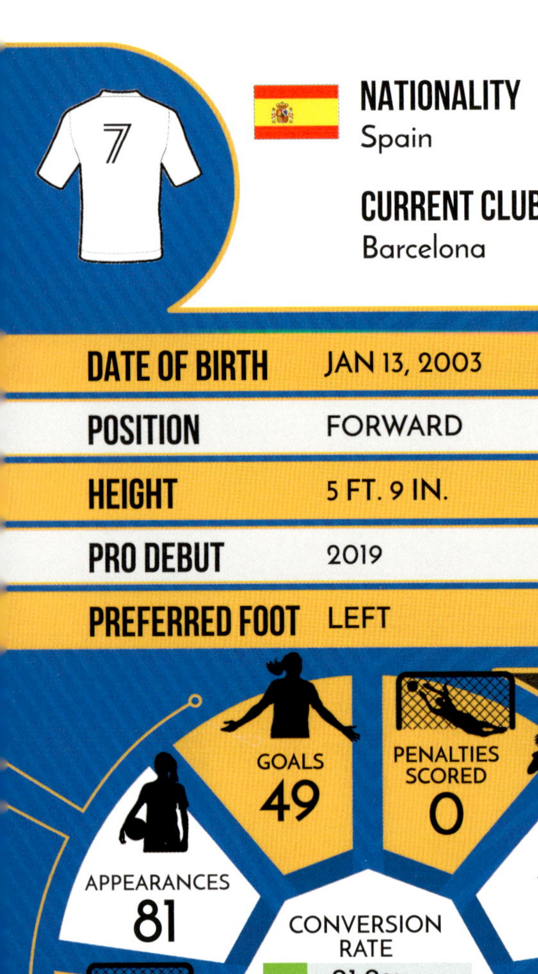

NATIONALITY
Spain

CURRENT CLUB
Barcelona

Just 19 years of age when she won a World Cup winner's medal, plus the tournament's Best Young Player Award, Salma Paralluelo has had a spectacular start to her career. Her mind-blowing dribbles into the penalty box, defence-splitting passes, and crosses put her among the world's very best attackers.

DATE OF BIRTH	JAN 13, 2003
POSITION	FORWARD
HEIGHT	5 FT. 9 IN.
PRO DEBUT	2019
PREFERRED FOOT	LEFT

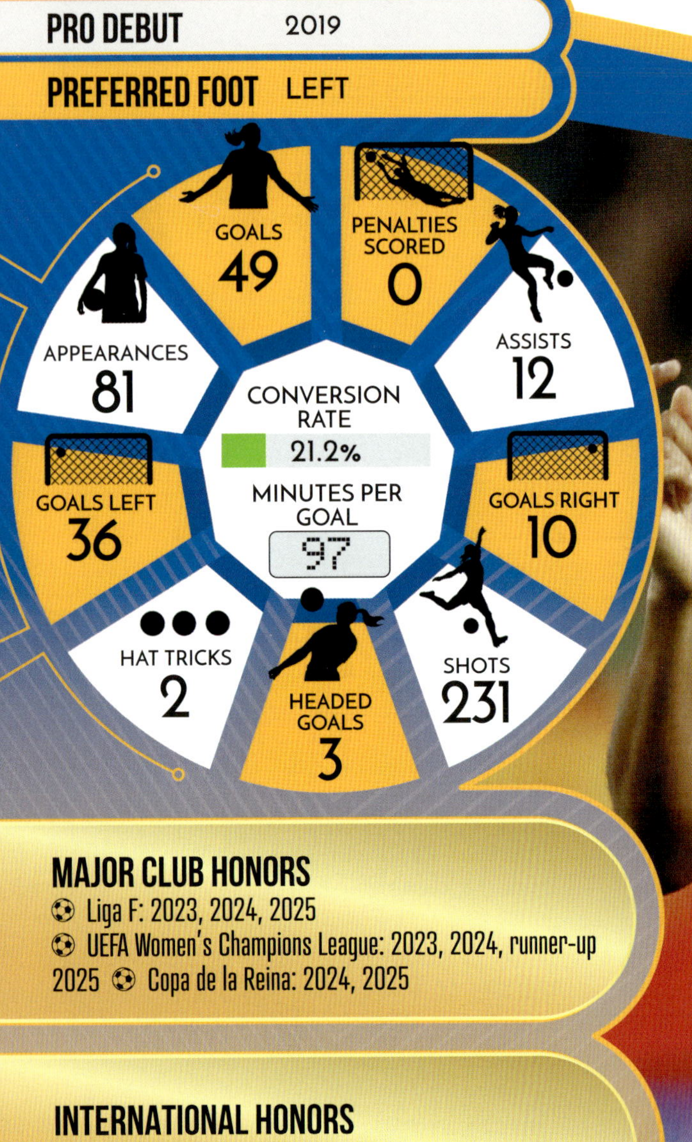

MAJOR CLUB HONORS

- Liga F: 2023, 2024, 2025
- UEFA Women's Champions League: 2023, 2024, runner-up 2025
- Copa de la Reina: 2024, 2025

INTERNATIONAL HONORS

- FIFA Women's World Cup: 2023
- UEFA Women's Nations League: 2024

ACTIVITY AREAS

ALEXANDRA POPP

Alexandra Popp has one of the most cultured left-footed shots in European soccer. A natural leader on the field, her aggression and passion are matched by high-level skill and creativity. Popp can burst through any defense and calmly put the ball past the goalkeeper.

NATIONALITY
Germany

CURRENT CLUB
VfL Wolfsburg

DATE OF BIRTH	APR 06, 1991
POSITION	STRIKER
HEIGHT	5 FT. 9 IN.
PRO DEBUT	2007
PREFERRED FOOT	LEFT

GOALS	37
PENALTIES SCORED	0
ASSISTS	21
GOALS RIGHT	3
SHOTS	248
HEADED GOALS	16
HAT TRICKS	1
GOALS LEFT	17
APPEARANCES	77
CONVERSION RATE	14.9%
MINUTES PER GOAL	154

MAJOR CLUB HONORS

⚽ Frauen-Bundesliga: 2013, 2014, 2017, 2018, 2019, 2020, 2022 ⚽ UEFA Women's Champions League: 2009 (Duisburg), 2013*, 2014* (*VfL Wolfsburg) ⚽ DFB-Pokal Frauen: 2009*, 2010* (*Duisburg), 2013, 2015-2023

INTERNATIONAL HONORS

⚽ Summer Olympic Games: Gold 2016
⚽ UEFA Women's Championship: Runner-up 2022

ACTIVITY AREAS

NATIONALITY
USA

CURRENT CLUB
Washington Spirit

TRINITY RODMAN

A hard-working forward who links well with other attackers, Trinity Rodman has already earned a reputation as a world class talent. She can quickly scan the field to make the best pass or spot a shooting opportunity, and is ice-cool in one-on-one situations with the keeper.

DATE OF BIRTH	MAY 20, 2002
POSITION	FORWARD
HEIGHT	5 FT. 8 IN.
PRO DEBUT	2021
PREFERRED FOOT	RIGHT

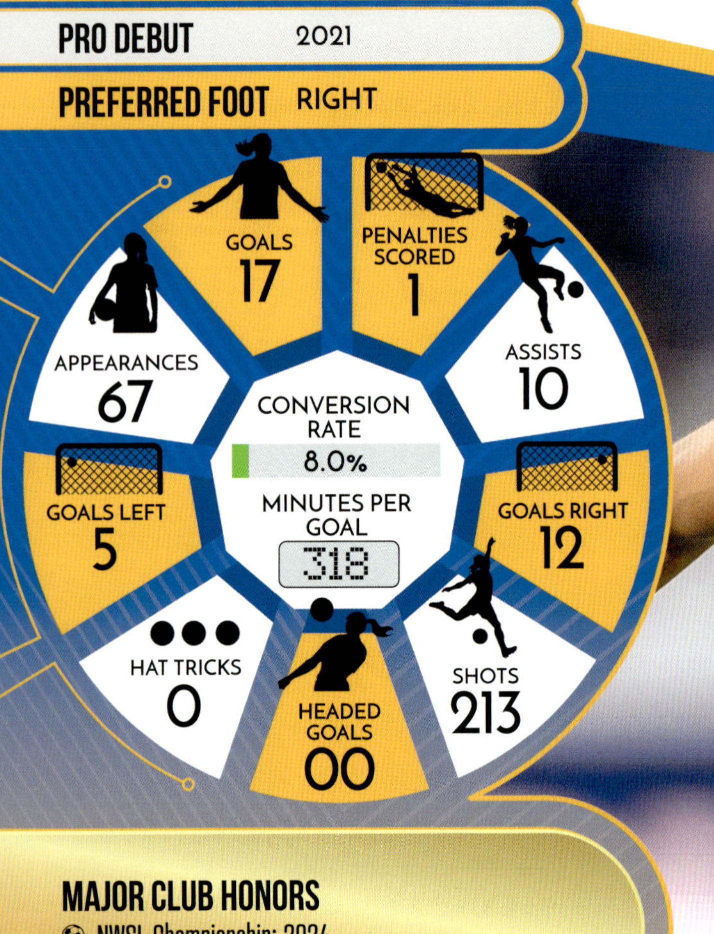

MAJOR CLUB HONORS

- NWSL Championship: 2024
- NWSL Challenge Cup: 2025

INTERNATIONAL HONORS

- Summer Olympic Games: Gold 2024
- CONCACAF Women's Championship: 2022
- CONCACAF Women's Gold Cup: 2024

ACTIVITY AREAS

FRIDOLINA ROLFÖ

The left-sided forward makes speedy runs out wide and has the awareness of when to cross into the penalty area or unleash a shot. Fridolina Rolfö is an aerial presence from free kicks and corners as she loses her marker and powers a header toward the net.

NATIONALITY
Sweden

CURRENT CLUB
Barcelona

DATE OF BIRTH	NOV 24, 1993
POSITION	FORWARD
HEIGHT	5 FT. 10 IN.
PRO DEBUT	2008
PREFERRED FOOT	LEFT

GOALS 25
PENALTIES SCORED 6
ASSISTS 17
GOALS RIGHT 8
SHOTS 108
HEADED GOALS 1
HAT TRICKS 0
GOALS LEFT 16
APPEARANCES 76

CONVERSION RATE 23.1%
MINUTES PER GOAL 200

MAJOR CLUB HONORS

⚽ Liga F: 2022, 2023, 2024, 2025 ⚽ UEFA Women's Champions League: 2023, 2024, runner-up 2025 ⚽ Frauen Bundesliga: 2020 (VfL Wolfsburg) ⚽ Copa de la Reina: 2022, 2024, 2025

INTERNATIONAL HONORS

⚽ Summer Olympic Games: Silver 2016, silver 2020 (2021)
⚽ FIFA Women's World Cup: Third place 2019, 2023

ACTIVITY AREAS

NATIONALITY
England

CURRENT CLUB
Arsenal

ALESSIA RUSSO

Alessia Russo's first role is to score goals, but her skill and vision make her much more than just a striker. She can operate in deeper areas to gain possession and then spray the ball effectively. Watch out for her clever flicks, twists, and spins that outfox defenders and beat goalkeepers.

DATE OF BIRTH	FEB 08, 1999
POSITION	STRIKER
HEIGHT	5 FT. 8 IN.
PRO DEBUT	2016
PREFERRED FOOT	RIGHT

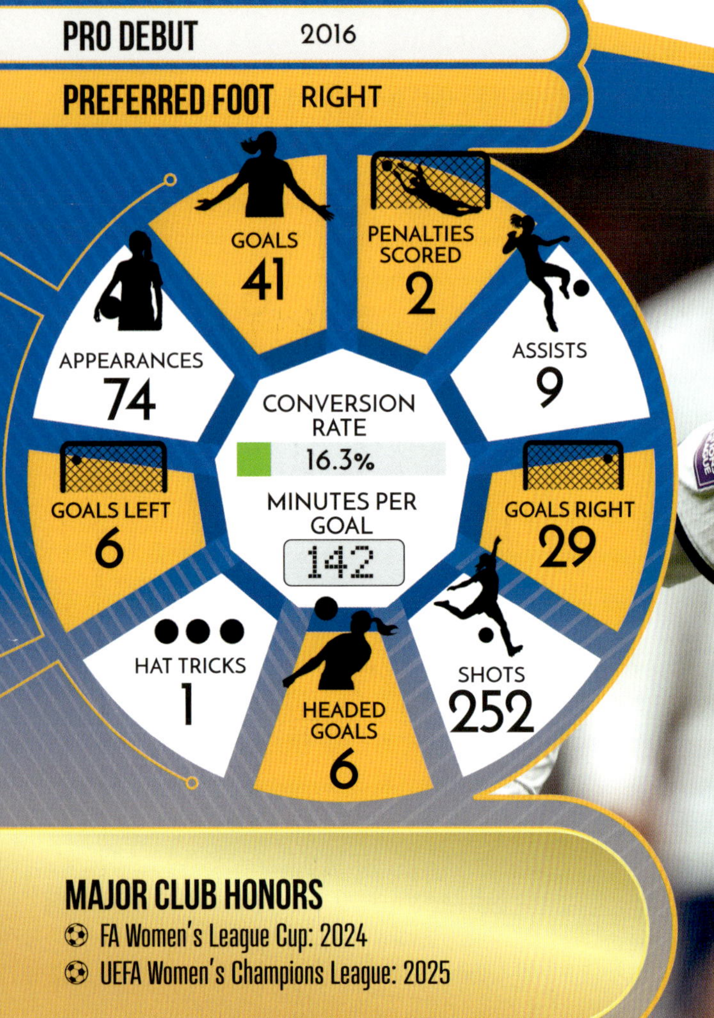

MAJOR CLUB HONORS

- FA Women's League Cup: 2024
- UEFA Women's Champions League: 2025

INTERNATIONAL HONORS

- UEFA Women's Championship: 2022
- UEFA Women's Finalissima: 2023
- FIFA Women's World Cup: Runner-up 2023

ACTIVITY AREAS

LEA SCHÜLLER

Lea Schüller enjoys the responsibility of being a top striker using her strength and expert hold-up skills to build forward momentum. Schüller's smart movement helps her find pockets of space in the opposition box, ready to time leaps over defenders and connect with a header.

NATIONALITY
Germany

CURRENT CLUB
Bayern Munich

DATE OF BIRTH	NOV 12, 1997
POSITION	FORWARD
HEIGHT	5 FT 8 IN.
PRO DEBUT	2013
PREFERRED FOOT	RIGHT

GOALS 41
PENALTIES SCORED 0
ASSISTS 13
APPEARANCES 85
CONVERSION RATE 19.4%
MINUTES PER GOAL 131
GOALS LEFT 5
GOALS RIGHT 20
HAT TRICKS 0
HEADED GOALS 15
SHOTS 211

MAJOR CLUB HONORS
- Frauen-Bundesliga: 2021, 2023, 2024, 2025
- DFB-Pokal Frauen: 2025

INTERNATIONAL HONORS
- UEFA Women's Championship: Runner-up 2022

ACTIVITY AREAS

NATIONALITY
USA

CURRENT CLUB
North Carolina Courage

JAEDYN SHAW

Averaging a goal every three games for the USA, the young Jaedyn Shaw is already exceling at the elite level. Versatile, athletic, and creative, Shaw is a superb team player who can quickly assess her options in the final third. She is hard to defend against, especially when she has an eye for goal.

DATE OF BIRTH	NOV 20, 2004
POSITION	FORWARD
HEIGHT	5 FT. 6 IN.
PRO DEBUT	2022
PREFERRED FOOT	RIGHT

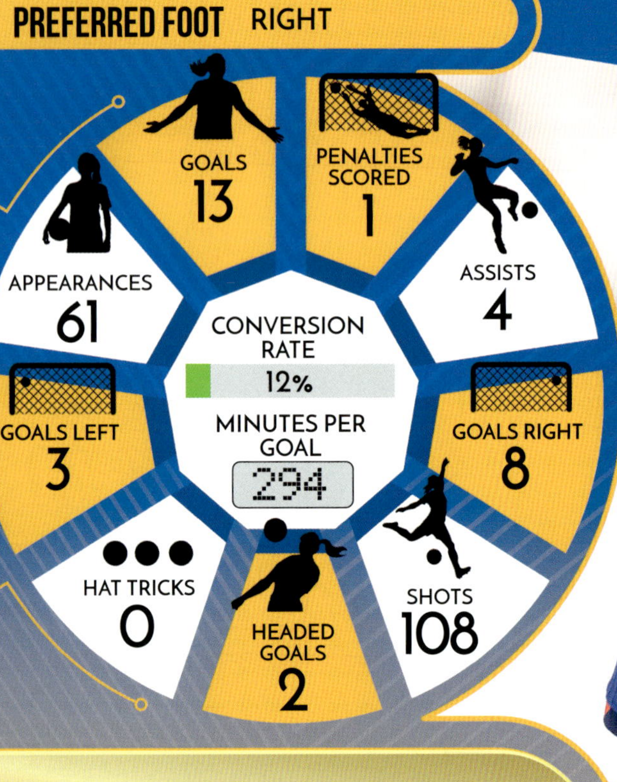

MAJOR CLUB HONORS
- NWSL Shield: 2023 (San Diego Wave)
- NWSL Challenge Cup: 2024 (San Diego Wave)

INTERNATIONAL HONORS
- CONCACAF Women's Gold Cup: 2024
- Summer Olympic Games: Gold 2024

ACTIVITY AREAS

KHADIJA SHAW

In 2024, Khadija "Bunny" Shaw netted her 68th goal in just 82 games for Manchester City to become the club's record scorer. Her speed and strength make her a menace in and around the box, and her power is difficult to contain, plus Shaw needs just a glimpse of the target to fire a shot away.

NATIONALITY
Jamaica

CURRENT CLUB
Manchester City

21

DATE OF BIRTH	JAN 31, 1997
POSITION	STRIKER
HEIGHT	5 FT. 11 IN.
PRO DEBUT	2018
PREFERRED FOOT	RIGHT

GOALS 56
PENALTIES SCORED 1
ASSISTS 11
GOALS RIGHT 24
SHOTS 268
HEADED GOALS 22
HAT TRICKS 5
GOALS LEFT 10
APPEARANCES 58
CONVERSION RATE 20.9%
MINUTES PER GOAL 80

MAJOR CLUB HONORS
- Women's League Cup: 2022
- Women's FA Cup: Runner-up 2022

INTERNATIONAL HONORS
- CONCACAF Women's Championship: Third place 2018, 2022

ACTIVITY AREAS

NATIONALITY
USA

CURRENT CLUB
Chicago Red Stars

MALLORY SWANSON

The adaptable Mallory Swanson is a gift to any manager. She can operate in a front two or lead the line as a sole number nine. The clinical strikeris capable of rifling shots home from any angle. Her 38 goals and 31 assists in 103 internationals is a testamement to her quality.

DATE OF BIRTH	APR 29, 1998
POSITION	FORWARD
HEIGHT	5 FT. 4 IN.
PRO DEBUT	2017
PREFERRED FOOT	RIGHT

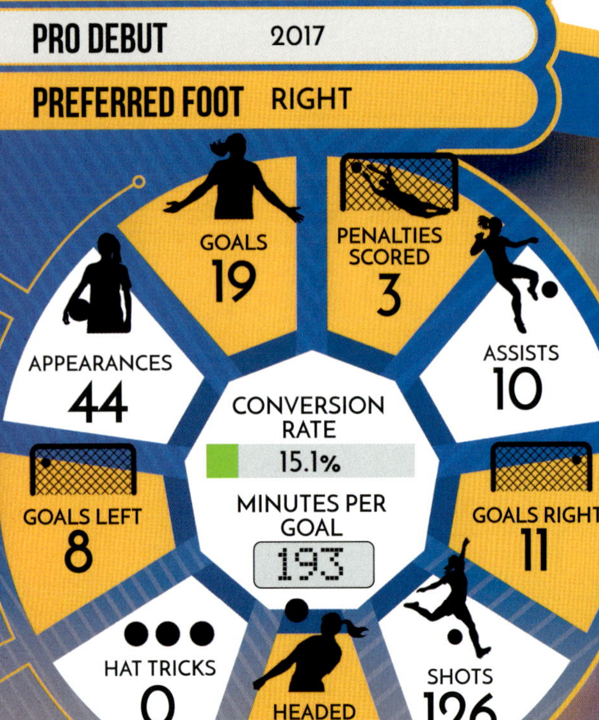

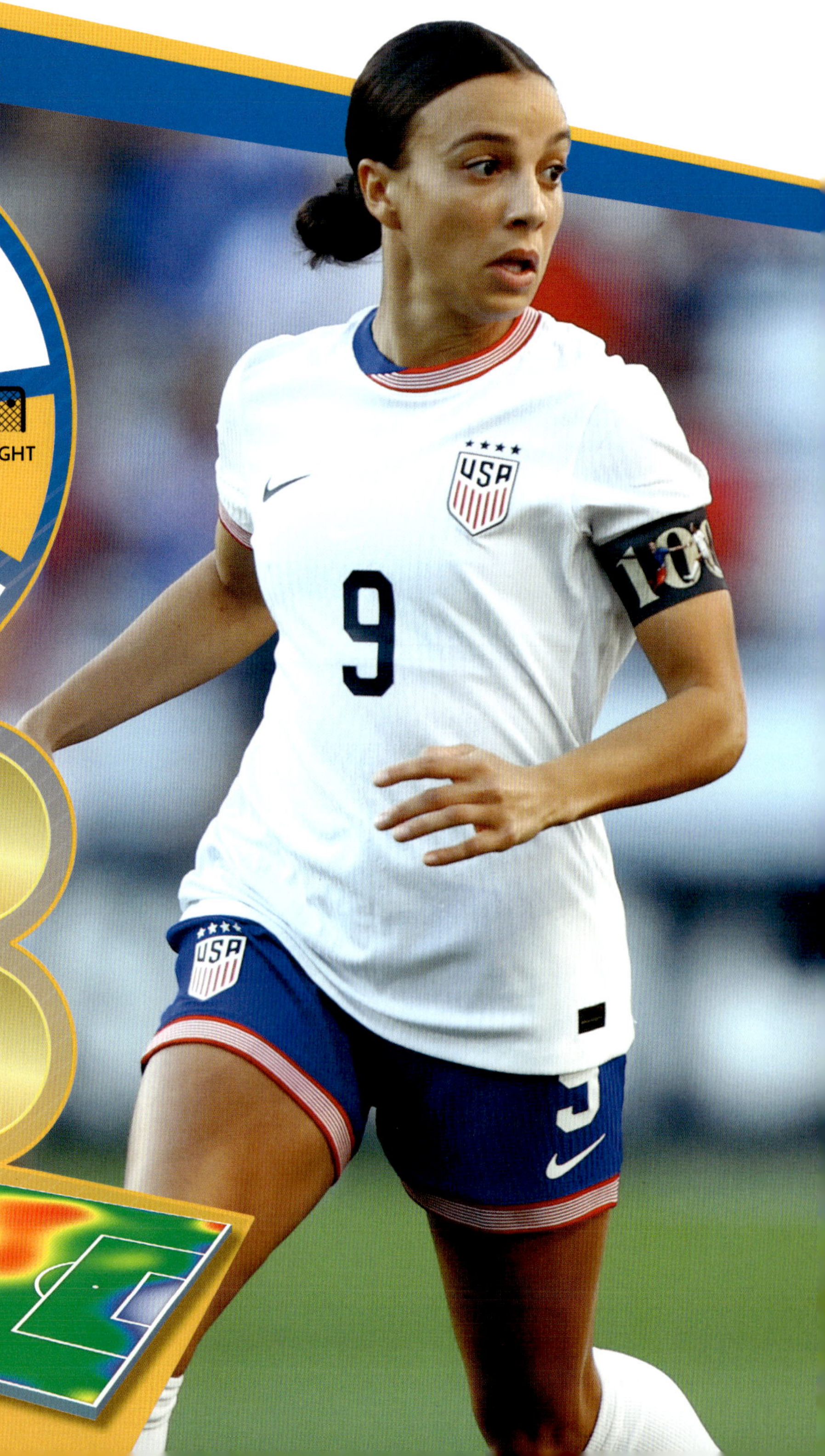

MAJOR CLUB HONORS

- None to date

INTERNATIONAL HONORS

- FIFA Women's World Cup: 2019
- Summer Olympic Games: Gold 2024
- CONCACAF Women's Championship: 2022

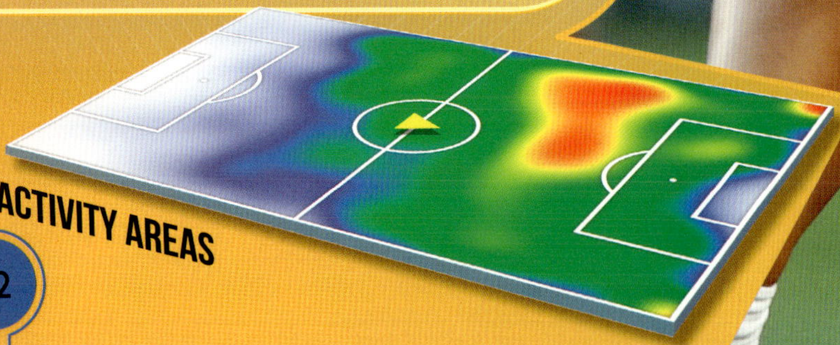

ACTIVITY AREAS

SOPHIA WILSON

Sophia Smith is an elite scorer who keeps on getting better. She keeps the ball under tight control with her dazzling right foot and has the explosive pace to get into prime positions. What's more, she is blessed with the shooting power and precision to test the goalkeeper.

NATIONALITY
USA

CURRENT CLUB
Portland Thorns

DATE OF BIRTH	AUG 10, 2000
POSITION	FORWARD
HEIGHT	5 FT. 6 IN.
PRO DEBUT	2020
PREFERRED FOOT	RIGHT

GOALS	38
PENALTIES SCORED	6
ASSISTS	14
GOALS RIGHT	23
SHOTS	279
HEADED GOALS	0
HAT TRICKS	2
GOALS LEFT	15
APPEARANCES	58
CONVERSION RATE	13.6%
MINUTES PER GOAL	120

MAJOR CLUB HONORS
- NWSL Championship: 2022
- NWSL Challenge Cup: 2021
- NWSL Shield: 2021

INTERNATIONAL HONORS
- CONCACAF Women's Championship: 2022
- CONCACAF Women's Gold Cup: 2024
- Summer Olympic Games: Gold 2024

ACTIVITY AREAS

GOALKEEPERS

While goal scorers win games, goalkeepers play a huge part in helping their team to protect a victory. As the last line of defense, their acrobatics and reflexes when faced with a goalbound shot can be the difference between winning and losing. A successful keeper uses all of her powers to command her penalty area and alongside agile and brave saves, she needs to have a strong kicking and throwing technique. No other position on the field depends on a single player or exerts the same pressure.

WHAT DO THE STATS MEAN?

CATCHES

This is the number of times the keeper has dealt with an attack–usually a cross or corner kick–by catching the ball.

CLEAN SHEETS

Any occasion on which the keeper has not let in a goal for the full duration of the game counts as a clean sheet.

GOALS CONCEDED

This is the number of goals the keeper has conceded across three seasons in top-division soccer.

PENALTIES FACED/SAVED

This is the number of times a keeper has faced a penalty (excludes shootouts) and how successful she has been at saving it.

PUNCHES

This is a measure of how often the keeper has dealt with a dangerous ball (usually a cross) by punching it clear.

SAVES

This shows how many times the goalkeeper has stopped a shot or header that was on target.

Did you know?

A penalty shootout—when each team takes penalties at the end of extra-time—is a dramatic event. A goalkeeper has the chance to be a hero by saving them and even, if needed, scoring a penalty herself.

NATIONALITY
Australia

CURRENT CLUB
Portland Thorns

MACKENZIE ARNOLD

The four clean sheets Mackenzie Arnold kept at the 2023 World Cup shows just how well she performs in high-stakes games. A confident catcher and puncher, she backs herself to save penalties too—and her record for both club and country bears testament to this special talent.

DATE OF BIRTH	FEB 25, 1994
POSITION	GOALKEEPER
HEIGHT	5 FT. 11 IN.
PRO DEBUT	2011
PREFERRED FOOT	RIGHT

MAJOR CLUB HONORS

- A-League Premiership: 2014 (Perth Glory), 2018 (Brisbane Roar)

INTERNATIONAL HONORS

- FIFA Women's World Cup: fourth-place 2023

ACTIVITY AREAS

ANN-KATRIN BERGER

The tall Ann-Katrin Berger commands her area superbly and communicates very effectively with her defense. Along with powerful goal-kicking abilities, one of her notable strengths is her concentration, pulling out quick-fire saves when she's faced with a snap shot.

NATIONALITY
Germany

CURRENT CLUB
Gotham FC

DATE OF BIRTH	OCT 09, 1990
POSITION	GOALKEEPER
HEIGHT	5 FT. 11 IN.
PRO DEBUT	2009
PREFERRED FOOT	RIGHT

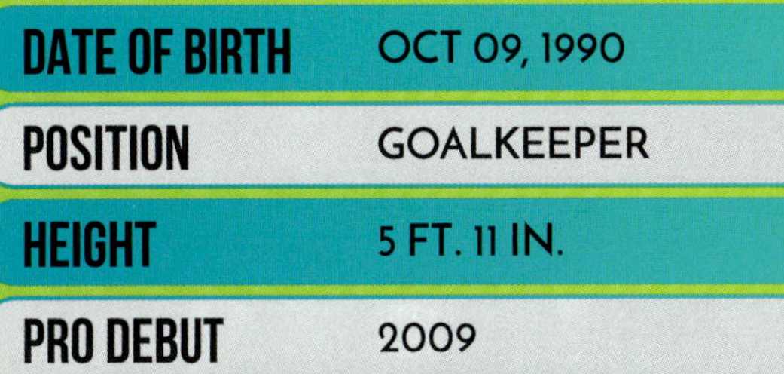

GOALS CONCEDED 53

APPEARANCES 63

PENALTIES SAVED 0

SAVES 165

CLEAN SHEETS 25

PENALTIES FACED 7

CATCHES 9

PUNCHES 26

MAJOR CLUB HONORS
⚽ Women's Super League: 2020, 2021, 2022, 2023, 2024 (all Chelsea) ⚽ UEFA Women's Champions League: Runner-up 2021 (Chelsea) ⚽ Women's FA Cup: 2021, 2022, 2023 (all Chelsea) ⚽ Frauen-Bundesliga: 2012 (Turbine Potsdam)

INTERNATIONAL HONORS
⚽ UEFA Women's Championship: Runner-up 2022

ACTIVITY AREAS

JANE CAMPBELL

NATIONALITY
USA

CURRENT CLUB
Houston Dash

An extremely consistent stopper, Jane Campbell was NWSL Goalkeeper of the Year in 2023. She is always alert in the box and is decisive when venturing forward to sweep danger away. She is confident dealing with crosses too, rising above her opponents to collect the ball.

DATE OF BIRTH	FEB 17, 1995
POSITION	GOALKEEPER
HEIGHT	5 FT. 9 IN.
PRO DEBUT	2017
PREFERRED FOOT	RIGHT

GOALS CONCEDED	95
APPEARANCES	76
CLEAN SHEETS	24
CATCHES	5
PUNCHES	25
PENALTIES FACED	13
PENALTIES SAVED	1
SAVES	280

MAJOR CLUB HONORS
- NWSL Challenge Cup: 2020

INTERNATIONAL HONORS
- CONCACAF Women's Gold Cup: 2024
- Summer Olympic Games: Bronze 2020 (2021)

ACTIVITY AREAS

CATALINA COLL

Catalina Coll made her Spain debut during the 2023 World Cup. Her talent and razor-sharp reflexes were on show from the round of 16 onward and she kept her place all the way to the final. Her style is to play out from the back and make perfect passes to beat the opponent's press and put her team on the attack.

NATIONALITY
Spain

CURRENT CLUB
Barcelona

DATE OF BIRTH	APR 23, 2001
POSITION	GOALKEEPER
HEIGHT	5 FT. 7 IN.
PRO DEBUT	2015
PREFERRED FOOT	RIGHT

MAJOR CLUB HONORS

⚽ Liga F: 2021, 2022, 2023, 2024, 2025 ⚽ UEFA Women's Champions League: 2021, 2023, 2024, runner-up 2025 ⚽ Copa de la Reina: 2021, 2022, 2025

INTERNATIONAL HONORS

⚽ FIFA Women's World Cup: 2023
⚽ UEFA Women's Nations League: 2024

ACTIVITY AREAS

MARY EARPS

27

NATIONALITY
England

CURRENT CLUB
Paris Saint-Germain

The technically brilliant Mary Earps makes difficult saves look easy. She catches and punches well too and transmits that confidence to her back four. She was the first goalkeeper to reach 50 clean sheets in the WSL before moving to France. Earps retired from the international team in 2025.

DATE OF BIRTH	MAR 07, 1993
POSITION	GOALKEEPER
HEIGHT	5 FT. 8 IN.
PRO DEBUT	2009
PREFERRED FOOT	RIGHT

GOALS CONCEDED 61
APPEARANCES 66
PENALTIES SAVED 0
SAVES 151
CLEAN SHEETS 31
PENALTIES FACED 3
CATCHES 14
PUNCHES 27

MAJOR CLUB HONORS

- Women's FA Cup: 2024 (Manchester Utd)
- Frauen-Bundesliga: 2019 (VfL Wolfsburg)
- DFB-Pokal Frauen: 2019 (VfL Wolfsburg)

INTERNATIONAL HONORS

- UEFA Women's Championship: 2022
- FIFA Women's World Cup: Runner-up 2023
- Women's Finalissima: 2023

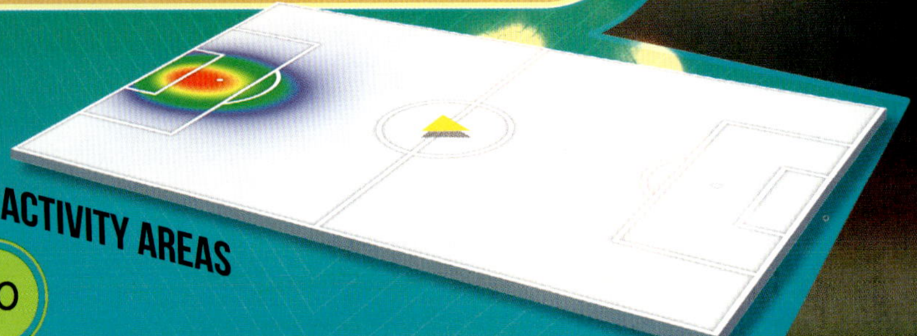

ACTIVITY AREAS

CHRISTIANE ENDLER

Acrobatic leaps for high balls and quick reflexes to block low shots make Christiane Endler super difficult to beat. Her tall, athletic frame gives her a huge advantage in one-on-one situations, where her world class reputation is most evident.

NATIONALITY
Chile

CURRENT CLUB
Lyon

DATE OF BIRTH	JUL 23, 1991
POSITION	GOALKEEPER
HEIGHT	6 FT.
PRO DEBUT	2008
PREFERRED FOOT	LEFT

MAJOR CLUB HONORS

⚽ Première Ligue (Division 1 Féminine): 2021 (PSG), 2022, 2023, 2024, 2025 ⚽ UEFA Women's Champions League: 2022, runner-up 2024 ⚽ Coupe de France Féminine: 2018 (PSG), 2023

INTERNATIONAL HONORS

⚽ Copa América Femenina Runner-up: 2018
⚽ Pan American Games: Silver 2023

ACTIVITY AREAS

NATIONALITY
Germany

CURRENT CLUB
VfL Wolfsburg

MERLE FROHMS

Relishing the battle to be the team's number one keeper, Merle Frohms rarely lets her performances drop. Aggressive but composed with her handling skills, combined with an ability to make passes like a cultured midfielder, she is the complete package between the posts.

DATE OF BIRTH	JAN 28, 1995
POSITION	GOALKEEPER
HEIGHT	5 FT. 9 IN.
PRO DEBUT	2012
PREFERRED FOOT	RIGHT

MAJOR CLUB HONORS

- Frauen-Bundesliga: 2013, 2014, 2017, 2018
- UEFA Women's Champions League: 2013, 2014
- DFB-Pokal Frauen: 2013, 2015, 2016, 2017, 2018

INTERNATIONAL HONORS

- UEFA Women's Championship: Runner-up 2022

ACTIVITY AREAS

MARIA LUISA GROHS

A first-class shot stopper with the positional intelligence to match, Maria Luisa Grohs is destined to be a goalkeeping hero for many seasons to come. She works hard to improve year over year, in particular when it comes to her fitness, kicking ability, and bravery on the pitch.

NATIONALITY
Germany

CURRENT CLUB
Bayern Munich

DATE OF BIRTH	JUN 13, 2001
POSITION	GOALKEEPER
HEIGHT	5 FT. 11 IN.
PRO DEBUT	2019
PREFERRED FOOT	RIGHT

MAJOR CLUB HONORS
- Frauen-Bundesliga: 2021, 2023, 2024, 2025
- DFB-Pokal Frauen: 2025

INTERNATIONAL HONORS
- None to date

ACTIVITY AREAS

NATIONALITY
England

CURRENT CLUB
Chelsea

HANNAH HAMPTON

A classy shot stopper, not only is Hannah Hampton blessed with great agility and quick reactions, but she has great distribution skills too, and can accurately kick or throw to a teammate to mount quick attacks. In 2024/25, Hampton became the youngest goalkeeper to make 100 WSL appearances.

DATE OF BIRTH	NOV 16, 2000
POSITION	GOALKEEPER
HEIGHT	5 FT. 8 IN.
PRO DEBUT	2017
PREFERRED FOOT	RIGHT

MAJOR CLUB HONORS
- Women's Super League: 2024, 2025
- Women's FA Cup: 2025
- Women's FA League Cup: 2025

INTERNATIONAL HONORS
- UEFA Women's Championship: 2022
- UEFA Women's Finalissima: 2023
- FIFA Women's World Cup: Runner-up 2023

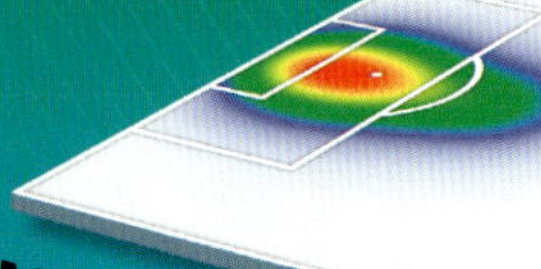

ACTIVITY AREAS

AUBREY RENEE KINGSBURY

NATIONALITY
USA

CURRENT CLUB
Washington Spirit

Goalkeepers aren't usually winners of the NWSL Championship MVP crown but Aubrey Kingsbury can boast that distinction. Besides her athleticism, the veteran goalkeeper is also a master at taking control of her penalty box and organizing her team to defend dangerous set pieces.

DATE OF BIRTH	NOV 20, 1991
POSITION	GOALKEEPER
HEIGHT	5 FT 9 IN.
PRO DEBUT	2014
PREFERRED FOOT	RIGHT

GOALS CONCEDED 97

APPEARANCES 77

PENALTIES SAVED 3

SAVES 227

CLEAN SHEETS 17

PENALTIES FACED 15

CATCHES 8

PUNCHES 28

MAJOR CLUB HONORS
- NWSL Championship: 2021
- NWSL Challenge Cup: 2025

INTERNATIONAL HONORS
- CONCACAF Women's Championship: 2022

ACTIVITY AREAS

CASEY MURPHY

NATIONALITY
USA

CURRENT CLUB
North Carolina Courage

Casey Murphy has already made her mark on the world stage, registering a formidable 15 clean sheets in her first 20 senior international games. A tall keeper, she has the reach and wrists to palm away shots and towers over opponents when collecting crosses.

DATE OF BIRTH	APR 25, 1996
POSITION	GOALKEEPER
HEIGHT	6 FT. 1 IN.
PRO DEBUT	2018
PREFERRED FOOT	RIGHT

GOALS CONCEDED 88
APPEARANCES 75
PENALTIES SAVED 1
CLEAN SHEETS 24
SAVES 222
PENALTIES FACED 8
CATCHES 10
PUNCHES 33

MAJOR CLUB HONORS
- NWSL Challenge Cup: 2022, 2023

INTERNATIONAL HONORS
- CONCACAF Women's Championship: 2022
- CONCACAF Women's Gold Cup: 2024
- Summer Olympic Games: Gold 2024

ACTIVITY AREAS

ZEĆIRA MUŠOVIĆ

Zećira Mušović has grown into a top keeper at Chelsea, battling for the role ahead of the team's other elite level stoppers. She is a super shot stopper, able to leap to the top corners and stretch low to push shots wide. She is known for her quick and accurate distribution too.

NATIONALITY
Sweden

CURRENT CLUB
Chelsea

DATE OF BIRTH	MAY 26, 1996
POSITION	GOALKEEPER
HEIGHT	5 FT. 11 IN.
PRO DEBUT	2011
PREFERRED FOOT	RIGHT

MAJOR CLUB HONORS

- Women's Super League: 2021, 2022, 2023, 2024, 2025
- Women's FA Cup: 2022, 2023, 2025
- Women's FA League Cup: 2021, 2025
- Damallsvenskan: 2013, 2014, 2015 (all FC Rosengard)

INTERNATIONAL HONORS

- FIFA Women's World Cup: third-place 2019, 2023
- Summer Olympic Games: Silver 2020 (2021)

ACTIVITY AREAS

NATIONALITY
USA

CURRENT CLUB
Chicago Stars

ALYSSA NAEHER

A two-time World Cup winner, Alyssa Naeher is lauded for her calm and composed presence in goal. She is a natural leader, good at organizing her defense to deal with set-piece threats, and inspires confidence in the rest of the team. Her athleticism, saving technique, and passing range are admirable.

DATE OF BIRTH	APR 20, 1988
POSITION	GOALKEEPER
HEIGHT	5 FT. 9 IN.
PRO DEBUT	2008
PREFERRED FOOT	RIGHT

GOALS CONCEDED 134
APPEARANCES 75
PENALTIES SAVED 1
SAVES 251
CLEAN SHEETS 17
PENALTIES FACED 14
CATCHES 6
PUNCHES 30

MAJOR CLUB HONORS

- None to date

INTERNATIONAL HONORS

- FIFA Women's World Cup: 2015, 2019
- CONCACAF Women's Championship: 2018, 2022
- CONCACAF W Gold Cup: 2024
- Summer Olympic Games: Gold 2024

ACTIVITY AREAS

CHIAMAKA NNADOZIE

Chiamaka Nnadozie's coaches praise her goalkeeping consistency and impact on the biggest stage. Never afraid to rush and smother the ball, or outjump opponents to make a catch, she remains Africa's premier stopper. She is an incredibly dependable player.

NATIONALITY
Nigeria

CURRENT CLUB
Paris FC

DATE OF BIRTH	DEC 08, 2000
POSITION	GOALKEEPER
HEIGHT	5 FT. 11 IN.
PRO DEBUT	2016
PREFERRED FOOT	RIGHT

GOALS CONCEDED 66

APPEARANCES 66

PENALTIES SAVED 4

SAVES 176

CLEAN SHEETS 28

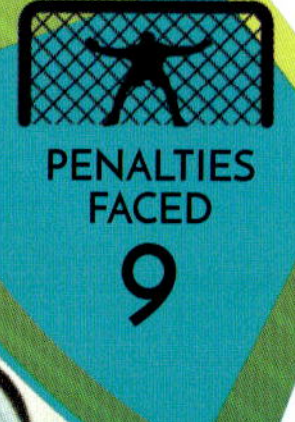
PENALTIES FACED 9

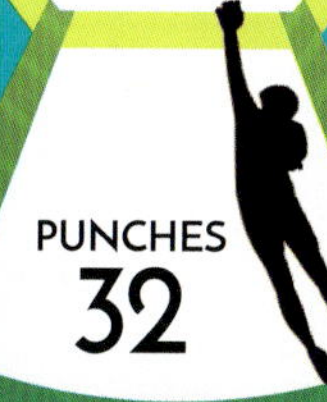
PUNCHES 32

CATCHES 4

MAJOR CLUB HONORS

- Coupe de France Féminine: 2025
- Nigerian Women's Championship: 2016 (Rivers Angels)
- Nigerian Women's Cup: 2016, 2017, 2018 (all Rivers Angels)

INTERNATIONAL HONORS

- African Women's Championships: 2018
- African Games: 2019

ACTIVITY AREAS

NATIONALITY
Spain

CURRENT CLUB
Club América

SANDRA PAÑOS

Modern goalkeepers must be assured with both their hands and feet, and Sandra Paños is a fine example. Comfortable leaving her area to link passes, she also has wonderful positioning that reduces her opponents' scoring chances. In 2024, she left Barcelona after nine seasons and now plays in the Mexican league.

DATE OF BIRTH	NOV 04, 1992
POSITION	GOALKEEPER
HEIGHT	5 FT. 7 IN.
PRO DEBUT	2010
PREFERRED FOOT	RIGHT

GOALS CONCEDED 27
APPEARANCES 46
PENALTIES SAVED 2
SAVES 64
CLEAN SHEETS 26
PENALTIES FACED 3
CATCHES 4
PUNCHES 7

MAJOR CLUB HONORS

⚽ Primera División: 2020, 2021, 2022, 2023, 2024 (all Barcelona) ⚽ UEFA Women's Champions League: 2021, 2023, 2024 (all Barcelona) ⚽ Copa de la Reina: 2017, 2018, 2020, 2021, 2022, 2024 (all Barcelona)

INTERNATIONAL HONORS

⚽ None to date

ACTIVITY AREAS

KAILEN SHERIDAN

Among Canada's best-ever sweeper-keepers, Kailen Sheridan is always aware of the play in front of her, ready to make passes that can open up a team. She is an imposing figure at the back, stopping headers and shots, or punching the danger clear if that is the best option.

NATIONALITY
Canada

CURRENT CLUB
San Diego Wave

DATE OF BIRTH	JUL 16, 1995
POSITION	GOALKEEPER
HEIGHT	5 FT. 10 IN.
PRO DEBUT	2013
PREFERRED FOOT	RIGHT

MAJOR CLUB HONORS
- NWSL Shield: 2023
- NWSL Challenge Cup: 2024

INTERNATIONAL HONORS
- Summer Olympic Games: Gold 2020 (2021)

ACTIVITY AREAS

NATIONALITY
Netherlands

CURRENT CLUB
Arsenal

DAPHNE VAN DOMSELAAR

Last season Daphne van Domselaar delivered unflappable performances in league, cup, and European fixtures to secure her spot as Arsenal's first-choice keeper. Her best qualities include catching and punching decisively when under pressure, and imposing herself on one-on-one situations.

DATE OF BIRTH	MAR 06, 2000
POSITION	GOALKEEPER
HEIGHT	5 FT. 9 IN.
PRO DEBUT	2017
PREFERRED FOOT	RIGHT

MAJOR CLUB HONORS
⚽ UEFA Women's Champions League: 2025 ⚽ Women's Eredivisie: 2019, 2021, 2022 (all Twente)

INTERNATIONAL HONORS
⚽ None to date

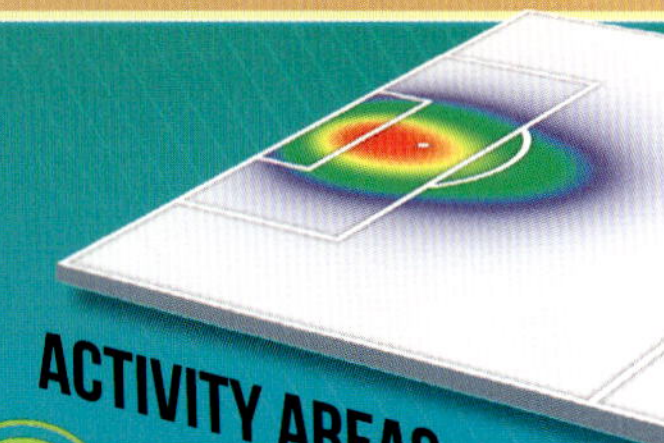

ACTIVITY AREAS

LYDIA WILLIAMS

Despite passing the 100 cap mark at international level, and a stellar career in the world's top leagues, Lydia Williams still wants to perform and win. She has safe hands when dealing with aerial threats and is good at anticipating shots, giving her a split second to react first.

NATIONALITY
Australia

CURRENT CLUB
Melbourne Victory

DATE OF BIRTH	MAY 13, 1988
POSITION	GOALKEEPER
HEIGHT	5 FT. 9 IN.
PRO DEBUT	2008
PREFERRED FOOT	RIGHT

MAJOR CLUB HONORS

⚽ A-League Championship: 2012 (Canberra United FC), 2020 (Melbourne City) ⚽ A-League Premiership: 2012, 2014 (all Canberra United FC), 2020 (Melbourne City)

INTERNATIONAL HONORS

⚽ Women's Asian Cup: 2010

ACTIVITY AREAS

MANAGERS

Although managers take no part on the field, their leadership behind the scenes is vital to how their team plays. Also known as the head coach, they pick the team for each game, deploy tactics, and decide substitutions. They plan how their squad trains, help buy and sell players, and speak to the media. The manager is the figurehead for their club. Take a look at the 12 in this section, the trophies they have won, and what puts them among the top coaches in women's soccer.

WHAT DO THE STATS MEAN?

GAMES MANAGED

This is the number of games the manager has been in charge of during the 2022/23 to 2024/25 seasons in top-flight soccer. For managers who operate (or operated) in the NWSL, the data relates to the 2022 to 2024 seasons.

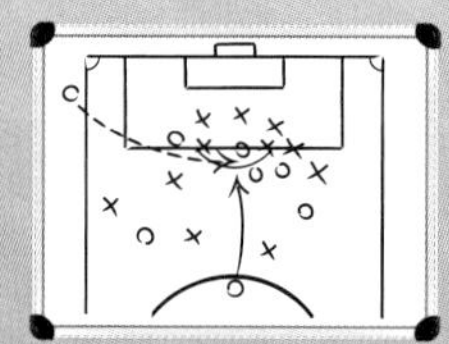

TEAMS MANAGED

The figure refers to the number of clubs (first teams only) the coach has managed during their career to date.

WINS, DRAWS, LOSSES

This is the number of games the coach has won, drawn, or lost during the three-season period, and includes one leg of a cup-tie, even if the tie was lost on aggregate or penalties.

TITLES AND TROPHIES

The three fields feature the manager's successes in the league, league cups, and intercontinental club competitions.

Did you know?

Sonia Bompastor switched from coaching Lyon to taking charge of Chelsea in 2024. She won three domestic trophies with the London club in her first season, including the WSL title in May 2025.

JUAN CARLOS AMORÓS

NATIONALITY
Spain

CURRENT CLUB
Gotham FC

Juan Carlos Amorós is extremely effective in improving players in his squad and turning a club's fortunes around. He demands an organized setup but with attacking opportunities that can be sprung the moment his team takes possession. Juan Carlos Amorós was the 2023 NWSL Coach of the Year.

YEARS AS HEAD COACH: 14

FIRST CLUB: TOTTENHAM WOMEN

CLUBS MANAGED	GAMES	LEAGUE TITLES
4	75	1
WINS	**DRAW**	**LOSSES**
38	19	18
CHAMPIONS LEAGUE TROPHIES	**OTHER TROPHIES**	
0	0	

*Excludes Super Cups

CAREER MAJOR HONORS
- NWSL Championship: 2023

SONIA BOMPASTOR

NATIONALITY
France

CURRENT CLUB
Chelsea

After eight years coaching Lyon's academy, Bompastor took charge of the first team with instant success. In 2022, she became the first to win the Women's Champions League as player and coach. The opposition can struggle to contain her team's flexibility between a 4-3-3 and 4-2-3-1 system. Bompastor joined Chelsea in 2024.

YEARS AS HEAD COACH: 4

FIRST CLUB: LYON

CLUBS MANAGED	GAMES	LEAGUE TITLES
2	97	4
WINS	**DRAW**	**LOSSES**
80	9	8
CHAMPIONS LEAGUE TROPHIES	**OTHER TROPHIES**	
1	5	

*Excludes Super Cups

CAREER MAJOR HONORS
- UEFA Women's Champions League: 2022, runner-up 2024 (all Lyon)
- WSL: 2025
- Women's FA Cup: 2025
- Women's FA League Cup: 2025
- Division 1 Féminine: 2022, 2023, 2024 (all Lyon)
- Coupe de France Féminine: 2023 (Lyon)
- Trophée des Championnes: 2022, 2023 (all Lyon)

JONAS EIDEVALL

NATIONALITY
Sweden

CURRENT CLUB
San Diego Wave

Passionate on the touchline, Eidevall is a technical coach who encourages his team to play out from the back. He also drills his players to press hard when not in possession of the ball. His attackers typically play out wide, tormenting full-backs and linking with a powerful central striker around the box.

YEARS AS HEAD COACH:	16
FIRST CLUB:	LUNDS BK

CLUBS MANAGED	GAMES	LEAGUE TITLES
4	68	3
WINS	**DRAW**	**LOSSES**
42	10	16
CHAMPIONS LEAGUE TROPHIES	**OTHER TROPHIES**	
0	3	

*Excludes Super Cups

CAREER MAJOR HONORS

- Damallsvenskan: 2013, 2014, 2019 (FC Rosengard)
- Women's FA League Cup: 2023, 2024 (all Arsenal)

JONATAN GIRÁLDEZ

NATIONALITY
Spain

CURRENT CLUB
Washington Spirit

Giráldez moved to coach in the NWSL in 2024 after turning Barcelona into a formidable team. His success in the Spanish league and Europe showed he could handle the pressure of coaching in the USA. Keeping possession, developing individual talent, and building a strong team ethos are his hallmarks.

YEARS AS HEAD COACH:	4
FIRST CLUB:	BARCELONA

CLUBS MANAGED	GAMES	LEAGUE TITLES
2	105	3
WINS	**DRAW**	**LOSSES**
89	7	9
CHAMPIONS LEAGUE TROPHIES	**OTHER TROPHIES**	
2	5	

*Excludes Super Cups

CAREER MAJOR HONORS

- NWSL Challenge Cup: 2025
- UEFA Women's Champions League: 2023, 2024 (all Barcelona)
- Liga F: 2022, 2023, 2024 (all Barcelona)
- Copa de la Reina: 2022, 2024 (all Barcelona)
- Supercopa de España: 2022, 2023, 2024 (all Barcelona)

LAURA HARVEY

NATIONALITY
England

CURRENT CLUB
Seattle Reign FC

With trophies in England and the USA, Laura Harvey focuses on small details that can make big differences during a game. Each player knows their role, in attacking and defending phases, and releasing wingers is often the route to how Laura Harvey beats teams who sit deep.

YEARS AS HEAD COACH: 18

FIRST CLUB: BIRMINGHAM CITY

CLUBS MANAGED	GAMES	LEAGUE TITLES
4	83	3

WINS	DRAW	LOSSES
32	19	32

CHAMPIONS LEAGUE TROPHIES	OTHER TROPHIES
0	7

*Excludes Super Cups

CAREER MAJOR HONORS

- NWSL Shield: 2014, 2015, 2022
- Women's Super League: 2011, 2012 (Arsenal)
- Women's Premier League: 2010 (Arsenal)
- Women's FA Cup: 2011 (Arsenal)

SEB HINES

NATIONALITY
England

CURRENT CLUB
Orlando Pride

Although Seb Hines was a defensive player in his playing career, his tactics and style of coaching with Orlando Pride allows for expansive and entertaining stuff. His team may press high against weaker opponents or use a low block to soak up pressure when facing stronger sides. A very talented young coach.

YEARS AS HEAD COACH: 3

FIRST CLUB: ORLANDO PRIDE

CLUBS MANAGED	GAMES	LEAGUE TITLES
1	75	1

WINS	DRAW	LOSSES
39	13	23

CHAMPIONS LEAGUE TROPHIES	OTHER TROPHIES
0	1

*Excludes Super Cups

CAREER MAJOR HONORS

- NWSL Shield: 2024
- NWSL Championship: 2024

JEFF HOPKINS

NATIONALITY
Wales

CURRENT CLUB
Melbourne Victory

The most successful coach in the A-League (formerly the W-League), Jeff Hopkins gets every drop of talent from his players. Blending experienced and exciting new prospects, the coach imparts great confidence in his team to beat any challenge in front of them with their well drilled and rehearsed tactics.

YEARS AS HEAD COACH: 26

FIRST CLUB: GIPPSLAND FALCONS

CLUBS MANAGED	GAMES	LEAGUE TITLES
3	69	0
WINS	**DRAW**	**LOSSES**
35	22	12
CHAMPIONS LEAGUE TROPHIES	**OTHER TROPHIES**	
N/A	0	

*Excludes Super Cups

CAREER MAJOR HONORS

- A-League: Premiers 2019
- A-League: Champions 2021, 2022
- A-League: Premiers 2009 (Brisbane Roar Women's)
- A-League: Champions 2009, 2011 (Brisbane Roar Women's)

ANTE JURIC

NATIONALITY
Australia

CURRENT CLUB
Sydney FC

Ante Juric's Sydney FC is extremely well set up for title challenges every year, being a strong defensive unit and possessing vision and spark in their attacks. His 4-3-3 style can convert to a back three if more numbers are needed in midfield to overpower opponents.

YEARS AS HEAD COACH: 8

FIRST CLUB: SYDNEY FC

CLUBS MANAGED	GAMES	LEAGUE TITLES
3	69	0
WINS	**DRAW**	**LOSSES**
35	12	22
CHAMPIONS LEAGUE TROPHIES	**OTHER TROPHIES**	
0	0	

*Excludes Super Cups

CAREER MAJOR HONORS

- A-League: Premiers 2021, 2022, 2023, 2024
- A-League: Champions 2019, 2023

JOE MONTEMURRO

NATIONALITY
Australia

CURRENT TEAM
Lyon

A master at instilling confidence into his players to express their individual skills as well as work for the team, Joe Montemurro is among the best coaches in the women's game. He prepares thoroughly for each match and can often make tweaks from the touchline to change the outcome in his team's favor.

YEARS AS HEAD COACH: 19

FIRST CLUB: SUNSHINE GEORGE CROSS

CLUBS MANAGED	GAMES	LEAGUE TITLES
3	84	4
WINS	**DRAW**	**LOSSES**
63	12	9
CHAMPIONS LEAGUE TROPHIES	**OTHER TROPHIES**	
0	5	

*Excludes Super Cups

CAREER MAJOR HONORS

- Première Ligue: 2025
- Serie A: 2022 (Juventus)
- Coppa Italia: 2022, 2023 (all Juventus)
- Women's Super League: 2019 (Arsenal)
- Women's FA League Cup: 2018 (Arsenal)

CASEY STONEY

NATIONALITY
England

CURRENT TEAM
Canadian Women's National Team

Casey Stoney followed her 2022 NWSL Coach of the Year by winning the Shield and Challenge Cup in the following two years. Her team is brave in possession, creating attacking patterns that force the opposition to chase and get behind the ball. In 2025, she left the NWSL to manage on the international stage.

YEARS AS HEAD COACH : 16

FIRST CLUB: CHELSEA

CLUBS MANAGED	GAMES	LEAGUE TITLES
3	61	1
WINS	**DRAW**	**LOSSES**
25	16	20
CHAMPIONS LEAGUE TROPHIES	**OTHER TROPHIES**	
0	2	

*Excludes Super Cups

CAREER MAJOR HONORS

- FA Women's Championship: 2019 (Manchester United)
- NWSL Shield: 2023 (San Diego Wave)
- NWSL Challenge Cup: 2024 (San Diego Wave)

ALEXANDER STRAUS

NATIONALITY
Norway

CURRENT CLUB
Angel City FC

Straus dominated the German league after joining Bayern in 2022, losing just one league game in his first two seasons. His style is to take early control of a game, instructing his team to overload the midfield and create scoring chances. Straus took his attacking style to Angel City FC in summer 2025.

YEARS AS HEAD COACH: 7

FIRST CLUB: NEST-SOTRA

CLUBS MANAGED	GAMES	LEAGUE TITLES
3	88	4
WINS	**DRAW**	**LOSSES**
68	12	8
CHAMPIONS LEAGUE TROPHIES	**OTHER TROPHIES**	
0	1	

*Excludes Super Cups

CAREER MAJOR HONORS

- Frauen Bundesliga: 2023, 2024 (all Bayern Munich)
- Toppserien: 2021, 2022 (all SK Brann)
- DFB-Supercu: 2024 (Bayern Munich)

TOMMY STROOT

NATIONALITY
Germany

CURRENT CLUB
VfL Wolfsburg

Tommy Stroot only turned 37 in 2025 but he already has an impressive career thanks to his skills on the training ground and gameday touchline. The German knows how to handle the demands of busy league and European schedules, having an organized 4-3-3 or 4-2-3-1 formation that creates lots of chances.

YEARS AS HEAD COACH: 12

FIRST CLUB: SV MEPPEN

CLUBS MANAGED	GAMES	LEAGUE TITLES
3	179	3
WINS	**DRAW**	**LOSSES**
139	17	23
CHAMPIONS LEAGUE TROPHIES	**OTHER TROPHIES**	
0	3	

*Excludes Super Cups

CAREER MAJOR HONORS

- Frauen Bundesliga: 2022
- DFB Pokal: 2022, 2023, 2024
- Women's Eredivisie: 2019, 2021 (Twente)

NOTES